If Gordon Bray wasn't actually born at the bottom of a rugby scrum, then surely the doctor who delivered him was a paid-up member of the Front Rowers Union. His name is synonymous with televised rugby union, his distinctive commentary style as much a part of the Australian game as Catchpole's passing or the Campese goose-step. Wherever the Wallabies are pulling on the sacred green and gold, Gordon is there. His passion for the game, its history, its personalities and trivia are a benchmark for anyone who loves the fifteen man code.

Like all good rugby men, Gordon is fond of his club, his drink, the odd wager and a good yarn. His encyclopaedic knowledge of the game's folklore is matched only by his staggering memory for rugby trivia—amassed from nearly thirty years in the business ... and irrepressibly passed on at some of the most awkward moments! Throughout the English-speaking world audiences have listened patiently to Gordon's trademark bursts of player biography while waiting to learn who's been awarded the feed.

Drawing on his ABC training as an all-round sports broadcaster, Gordon calls a wide range of events—from lawn bowls and yacht racing to athletics, cricket and golf. He is chief rugby caller for the Seven Network and writes a weekly rugby column for the *Daily Telegraph*. And they pay him to do it!

Gordon is married with two young children and lives in Sydney.

By the same author

The Rugby Laws Explained (Ed)
The Spirit of Rugby—A Tribute to Rugby Union (Ed)

From The Ruck

Gordon BRAY

RANDOM HOUSE
A U S T R A L I A

Random House Australia Pty Ltd
20 Alfred Street, Milsons Point, NSW 2061
http://www.randomhouse.com.au

Sydney   New York   Toronto
London   Auckland   Johannesburg
and agencies throughout the world

National Library of Australia
Cataloguing-in-Publication Data

Bray, Gordon.
From the ruck: a commentator tells all.

ISBN 0 09 183055 9.

1. Rugby Union football—Australia. I. Title.

796.3330994

10 9 8 7 6 5 4 3 2 1

Design by Phil Campbell, Melbourne
Typeset by Midland Typesetters, Maryborough, Victoria
Printed by Griffin Paperbacks, Adelaide

Acknowledgements

As celebrated British rugby officianado Cliff Morgan rightly states later in this book, 'Nick Farr-Jones was the greatest player in the world'. I was honoured when an Australian sporting hero of Nick's standing unhesitatingly agreed to write the Foreword to *From the Ruck*.

Whether as magnanimous skipper or outstanding player, he was an inspiration to team-mates and country. Since retiring from international rugby in 1992 after sixty three Tests for the Wallabies, Nick's professional career path has blossomed in Paris with France's leading bank, Société Générale. The Farr-Jones clan, too, has expanded its horizons in Europe—Nick and Angie are now parents to three beautiful young children. What with the timely arrivals of their first son Benjamin and Jean-Luc Poidevin here in Sydney, our World Cup prospects in 2019 have received a healthy boost!

Special thanks are also extended to David Salter, former Head of ABC TV Sport. His support and encouragement when this project was first mooted back in 1992 was the catalyst to press ahead.

I must also express gratitude to my long-suffering wife Catherine and our young children Andrew and Anna. Their support, patience and understanding during those frequent vigils at my computer have provided ongoing strength and comfort.

Lastly, I'd like to dedicate this book to one of the legends of Australian rugby. During my formative years at the ABC, I was extremely fortunate to spend many Saturday evenings with the late Cyril Towers at the old Gladstone Hotel, Darlinghurst. Thankfully his wisdom and passion live on through the famous 'Howard' rugby name.

Contents

REMINISCENCE AND REFLECTION

Foreword

It was yet another of those uniquely memorable experiences that only rugby can provide. The night had begun without any great expectations. Just a typical Sunday night celebration in Hong Kong after yet another successful Sevens tournament. Gordon Bray and myself (having concluded our broadcasting duties) had drained enough lagers to feel like 'one more for the road' before turning in for the night. In search of the proverbial last watering hole, we were wandering around the Hilton Hotel and bumped into Waisale Serevi, Fiji's broad-smiling master of the sevens game.

After a hearty slap on the back and the ritual cursing of New Zealand's good fortune earlier in the day, Serevi wondered whether we'd like to join him and his team-mates upstairs for a modest cup of kava. What better way could there be to wash down the preceding beers? Gordon and I were soon seated cross-legged among the entire Fiji Sevens squad in a tiny hotel room. The next few hours were spent singing Island songs and passing around the sacred bowl of muddy water as batch after batch of kava was prepared in the large plastic bucket the Fijians had thoughtfully brought along. With mouths now numb from the brew I swear that by the wee hours of the morning both Gordon and I had become fluent in Fijian and could harmonise as sweetly as any Suva pop star.

The extraordinary spirit and experience of becoming honorary Fijians for that night will remain with Gordon and myself for life. Yet it was only one of a multitude of wonderful memories the game of rugby offers. *From the Ruck* is a highly entertaining sampling of many more of those unique moments as they were enjoyed—and are now recounted—by Gordon through his distinguished career as a sports broadcaster and commentator.

I'm sure that those who don't know Gordon personally still get a feel for his passion for sport (and rugby in particular) from his enthusiastic commentary style. As you read this book you may come to realise that the passion is more of an obsession. Gordon himself admits that rugby is an addiction and that a large part of his life is spent searching for the next 'fix'. Judging by many of the stories he tells in these pages, those journeys may have been long—but not particularly arduous.

Many of the paths for Gordon were trodden on tour with the Wallabies. No doubt he would agree with the old Wallaby adage that rugby touring is a bit like sex and chocolate cake: when it's good it's *fantastic*, but when it's bad, well, it's still pretty good. A small number of the journalists who've accompanied touring Wallaby sides became good friends of the team. Gordon has always been in that number. Highly respected at his craft, I think it was his special enthusiasm for both the game and the Wallabies' fortunes that endeared him to the troops on tour after tour.

More importantly for the players and administrators, Gordon has always been regarded as someone who could be trusted. This gave him automatic entry into the team's 'inner sanctum'. But this did not translate (as it so easily could have) into biased commentary. Despite his natural desire to see the national team prevail, Gordon always commentates—and now writes—exactly as he sees things. As we Aussies like to say, he calls a spade a bloody shovel, which makes interesting insights while re-reading some of the interviews he's conducted over the years.

Reflecting for a moment on the Wallabies' World Cup success in 1991, one of the most rewarding aspects for me was the enthusiasm it generated among the youngsters back home. Junior rugby registrations sky-rocketed the following year. No doubt much of this was the result of our style of play and ultimate victory. But now I've been involved in some rugby broadcasting myself I also understand that the snowballing interest and support back in Australia can be credited to the live telecasts and the commentary team—headed, of course, by Gordon. It was they who re-created the match atmosphere in the living rooms of all those aspiring Campeses, Littles and Horans.

From the Ruck is a most entertaining armchair ride through Gordon's life and experiences as a sports broadcaster. There is much more to sample here than rugby, but it is difficult to avoid comparing his career to that of the new breed of professional rugby players. Like them he's being paid to do something that, if the opportunity and privilege arose, they'd jump at for nothing. Wouldn't we all? No wonder these recollections are so colourful and enjoyable, Gordy!

Nick Farr-Jones
France, April 1997

Years ago a friend sent me a wonderful quotation from *The Enquirer's Oracle*, published in 1883. Paragraph 1368 reads:

'Football should be denounced, without qualification, as a brutal, savage, and insane pastime.'

The anonymous aphorist was clearly someone who's seen the bottom of a ruck, first hand.

Introduction—the Essence of Rugby

Anyone with more than a passing interest in the sport knows that rugby is much more than a game. But what, precisely, is it that gives rugby its special qualities? For me it's no single thing but the sum of its remarkably diverse parts—its history, its personalities, its social life. If we are foolish enough to attempt a definition of rugby's essence, then these three aspects of the game deserve equal attention.

SEVENTY years ago the prospect of rubbing shoulders with royalty was pretty daunting, especially to a raw-boned Australian farmer on tour with the celebrated 1927–28 Waratah rugby team. So, before the players were due to present themselves at the gates of Buckingham Palace, he slipped off to a local hostelry and fortified himself with a pint or three of the publican's Best Bitter.

An hour later, the audience with George V was going well. Always a proud father, the King asked for his beloved Elizabeth, the Princess Royal, to be wheeled into the room for the visiting antipodean rugby team to admire. Our well-primed Waratah was overcome by a rush of paternal instinct and boldly asked his monarch whether he could nurse the child. After some initial reluctance, the request was surprisingly granted.

For a while the Waratah was happy just to cradle the infant Elizabeth in his massive forearms. But, with his inhibitions dissolved by the Best Bitter, it wasn't long before he tossed the baby in the air like a football. The whole room watched in disbelief as the tiny Princess soared towards the high Palace ceiling and tumbled giggling back down into those sure farmer's hands.

The King said not a word. (No doubt he was silently praying his guest wouldn't now try a kick for touch.) In that one brief moment the future Queen had been anointed with the 'spirit of rugby'—Australian style.

At Twickenham more than sixty years later she would hand the William Webb-Ellis Trophy to Nick Farr-Jones, captain of the World Cup-winning Wallabies. The circle was complete. (And Nick didn't drop it, either.)

My first contact with rugby was as a youngster watching the ABC's weekly *Match of the Day* telecasts of the Sydney club competition. Legendary commentator Norman 'Nugget' May would describe the game concisely in the best ABC tradition, but he also managed to convey just a hint of expectation and enthusiasm. Alongside Norman was the immortal 'expert' Cyril Towers, who was always complaining about the over-inflated footballs. In hindsight he was right, but back then his pleas fell on deaf ears.

Randwick, the 'Galloping Greens', invariably seemed to feature in these misty black-and-white telecasts. Perhaps that was because the welcoming bar of the Randwick Rugby Union Football Club was just across the road from Coogee Oval (after all, television crews are as fond of a drink as the next bloke). The more likely explanation was that the Randwick first-grade side was virtually 24-carat Wallaby. They were all either current Wallabies, ex-Wallabies, or soon-to-be Wallabies.

Of all those great players who'd pulled on the Australian jumper it was Ken Catchpole who stood out. He was a sportsman of extraordinary skill and sheer instinctive brilliance: always there in the firing line, always creating something magical, always the maestro. To me he is the greatest rugby player this nation has produced. 'Catchy' later became an expert commentator with ABC Radio. It was a thrill to eventually work alongside my boyhood hero—a man of humility and strong principles whose tactical insights were a continuing revelation.

But I digress. Does Australian rugby have a definable 'essence'?

Fifty years ago, in his delightful *From Days Without Sunset*, Denzil Bachelor observed that the Australian attitude to sport was 'dour, grim and puritanical' in all games—except one. 'They relax into light-heartedness and schoolboy zest when they pull on their boots for rugby football,' Truly said, although some might suggest that the *real* 'zest' kicks in when they finally hang those boots up!

Rugby is an addiction. Not just the sport itself but the way of life which supports the game. Millions of disciples world-wide live for their next 'fix'. For me, one of my more unusual addictive experiences occurred in the fertile farming country of south-western New South Wales.

It's around 2 a.m.—the night is still young. The setting is the Murrumbidgee Gentlemen's Club. In true Australian style there isn't a gentleman or a club anywhere to be seen. Some time ago—a distant memory—I sang for my supper as the guest speaker at the annual black-tie presentation dinner of the Wagga Agricultural College Rugby Club. Now, with eighty of the survivors, I'm perched on the riverbank under a weeping willow, nursing a beer while the drizzle gently ruins my new Italian designer dinner suit.

Who cares? Somewhere in the darkness I can just hear the contented breathing of a herd of well-nourished cattle. The satisfying hiss of a newly-tapped keg pierces the damp air. The serious drinking is about to begin. There is laughter and conversation from the silhouettes all around me. The girls have mysteriously managed to shed their evening gowns in favour of rugby jumpers and jeans. Despite the rain someone is tending a small bonfire, I suspect more for the comforting crackle than any warmth it affords.

All the talk is rugby. 'What's David Campese *really* like?' Everyone, the women included, wants to share rugby experiences and ask me questions about the game at the international level. My presence is acknowledged, but as an equal. A fresh schooner of beer is thrust in my hand every ten minutes. Meanwhile, the mud is dissolving my posh new Lloyds slip-ons.

It doesn't matter. This is something special: one of those suspended moments of uncomplicated friendship only rugby seems able to provide. Heartfelt, unifying—and fun.

By 4 a.m. the numbers have somehow swollen and the bonfire is roaring. The party is really bubbling now, but hard-earned experience tells me it's time to beat a dignified retreat. Five hours later my plane begins its descent into Sydney. I feel a terrible tug of regret and nostalgia as the tarmac rushes up towards me and I re-enter the real world.

At the core of this magic thing we call the 'essence of rugby' is the unique physical quality of the game itself. Put plainly, rugby demands bravery of its players, whether you're an anonymous lower-grade 'subbie' or a celebrated International. The best players can all summon strong mental focus to match their personal courage. It is no surprise to learn that when the Empire rallied its sons to arms the 'game they play in heaven' responded to the call. The horrors of the Great War robbed us of too many of the world's finest rugby players. Their legacy remains an integral and honoured part of our rugby heritage.

Eighty years after those terrible sacrifices, the long campaign to preserve the amateur status of the game at the elite level is over. The cherished Corinthian ethic of the 'gentleman' rugby player is all but dismantled. Yet despite the legions of doom-sayers, rugby has survived these winds of change, and will do so again.

Long after the final scores and statistics are forgotten it is the exuberant single moments of rugby genius which live so strongly in the memory. We may have seen them as schoolboys, but can still recall each one in minute detail. One inspired pass, a dazzling step, towering punt, unstoppable shove. Somehow, through its inspired design, rugby simultaneously allows for explosions of dazzling individual brilliance and equally memorable passages of Herculean team endeavour.

George Gregan achieved instant international celebrity with his astonishing tackle in Sydney on Jeff Wilson to secure the 1994 Bledisloe Cup match for Australia. It was a remarkable climax to an epic Test.

Back in 1948, another Wallaby performed a similarly heroic deed. With 70,000 English fans leaping to their feet at Twickenham, D.W. Swarbrick sprinted clear of the Australian defence and dived into the in-goal area to complete what looked like a match-winning try. But before he could force the ball, 'a pin-pointed rocket caught him, swept him through mid-air, ball and all, and into the no-man's-land of touch in goal'. Wallaby captain Trevor Allan, in a super human feat driven by forlorn hope, had saved his side when all seemed lost.

For some, these moments of glory in the rugby spotlight are fleeting. In 1978 Greg Cornelsen found a good excuse to shave off his beard—four good reasons, in fact. He'd just scored four tries in the Wallabies' gruelling 30–16 win at Eden Park. Remarkably, the mild-mannered New England farm boy went on to play twenty-five Tests—and remained tryless in the other twenty-four!

Sheer audacity can also be rewarded with a lasting niche in rugby folklore. The late Darryl Haberecht, former Wallaby coach and devotee of improvisation, masterminded the famous 'up the jumper' try scored by NSW Country against the Sydney side in their 1975 grudge match.

Haberecht's inspired stratagem of actually hiding the ball until you got it over the line was promptly outlawed by the International Rugby Board as not being within the spirit of the game. I beg to differ. It is *precisely* that kind of eccentric innovation which helps define the real essence of rugby.

• •

The spirit of rugby has always embraced some quaint traditions, but perhaps none more peculiar than a weekly ritual of the Sydney competition's Southern Districts Rebels.

Nine stuffed dolls are suspended by string from the ceiling of their clubhouse. Each represents one of the club's senior teams, from first-grade down to the under 19s.

If a side loses, then its relevant doll is turned upside down (or sideways for a draw). Any thirsty patron arriving at the club after 5 p.m. on a Saturday need only glance up at this instant ready-reckoner to learn of the club's fortunes that day.

• •

Rugby
Reportage

'Mercy loosens the law'. Barrister Adrian Stoop was capped 15 times for England but only gained lasting notoriety when he retired as a player and took up the whistle. In a Barbarians vs East Midlands fixture he somehow managed to blow full time after only 68 minutes of play. The irate crowd expressed its displeasure in such an ungentlemanly (but effective) manner that the bemused players were forced to return from the dressing rooms and complete the match

Quarter-final Fever

Preparing for a commentary on a rugby international is no different from a school examination, although I know which I'd prefer. Good preparation should equate to a good performance. Much of the hard work might never be used 'on air', but every now and then it's the detailed preparation that saves the day.

BEFORE a big game, I like to lock myself away with research material. Usually it's part of a three- to four-day build-up. This period includes attendance at training sessions, observing the application and the mood of the players, memorising my background notes and speaking to as many relevant people as possible.

For example, the usually anonymous team physiotherapist is often a good person to consult. Through a long international campaign the Wallabies' 'physio' Greg Craig would see and hear much more of the players than their wives and girlfriends. When a clearly distressed Phil Kearns hobbled off in the match against Argentina early in the 1991 World Cup the press wrote the injury up as a major setback for Australia. Greg told us it was no more than an ankle strain so we could confidently predict that the big No. 2 would be fit for the next crucial game.

During that World Cup campaign in Britain and Ireland it became a matter of 'eating and sleeping' rugby for the ABC team. This really paid off for us during the hectic period of the quarter-finals.

On the Saturday we began with a live telecast from Murrayfield of Scotland's clash with Western Samoa. The previous day I'd made an impromptu visit to the Samoans' hotel where the team room was plastered with faxes from all over the world. The manager greeted me and then sat down with his guitar and burst into a stirring rendition of the 'sixties' song 'Knights in White Satin'. I felt very privileged to be there and was able to glean some useful background information on the team.

The whole experience of getting to know these Pacific crusaders helped the tone and detail of my call. They were gallant losers after a typically spirited contest and I can still recall feeling a tinge of sadness that the Samoan fairytale had ended.

But events swiftly overtook those emotions. The second quarter-final of the day—France v England in Paris—was scheduled to begin shortly after the Scotland game. The ABC had planned to use the English 'call' over French pictures, but as we were packing up our commentary position I got a message through the headphones that there was no audio—let alone commentary—coming through with the pictures from Paris. Could we please stay and provide the call? It was precisely one of those situations where I would have to rely on all the preparation I'd done over the previous months.

So, with the temperature hovering just above zero the ABC commentary team of Messrs Bray, Pearse and Handy proceeded to call the whole game watching a tiny monitor high in the Murrayfield grandstand. The technique is known as an 'off-tube' call, but it's usually done from the comfort of a warm television studio. Our teeth were chattering as streams of cold Scots air came up through the floor. Chris Handy had left his coat at the hotel and by half-time was suffering mild frostbite.

It was a weird feeling broadcasting a game at an empty stadium in fading light. In fact, the telecast finished in darkness as we continued to consult my notes and team sheets by torchlight. After four hours of virtually non-stop commentary we then jumped on the next flight to Dublin for Australia's quarter-final against Ireland. As we shared a warming drink somewhere over the north of England, none of us could have imagined that even more dramatic events awaited at Lansdowne Road.

Without question that contest ranks as the most dramatic of my broadcasting career. With eight minutes remaining the Wallabies were clinging to a three-point lead. Then disaster. Gordon Hamilton swooped onto John Clarke's pass and the twenty-seven-year-old shipping executive from Belfast scored what seemed to be the match-winning try. The ABC commentary team was so stunned that we didn't utter a single syllable for thirty-one long seconds. Euphoria gripped the Irish fans and they produced a glorious, prolonged cheering sound like no other I've heard at any sporting event.

It's now history that the Australians had the courage, composure and presence of mind to hit back with a brilliantly executed 'last-ditch' try by acting captain Michael Lynagh (who'd first toured Britain and Ireland with the 1981–82 unbeaten Australian Schoolboys team). Back home in Australia it was around 3 a.m., but we were told later that hundreds of thousands of fans had stayed up to witness the Wallabies snatch this improbable victory.

The 1991 World Cup champions had literally been seconds away from an early flight home. I spoke to Australian centre Richard Tombs that night and asked if he could remember his first thought when Hamilton scored.

'Easy,' Tombs replied. 'I thought, "I'm not going to be able to wash and dry my dirty clothes in time for tomorrow morning's flight back to Australia!"' And that delightfully candid admission was exactly the type of information to be tucked away and brought out again as part of our preparation for the next match.

• •

Which recently-retired player managed three tries in a single match at Twickenham, but no-one in the crowd actually saw them scored because of an impenetrable pea-soup fog?

Can't remember? Here's a hint. This same legend of modern Australian rugby was also Wallaby vice-captain in a Bledisloe Cup series at the age of just twenty and is now Global Head of Financial Markets for Westpac.

The answer, of course, is Michael Hawker. 'Hawk-Eye' returned to the centre of local rugby as chairman of the three-man Australian selection panel in 1996.

(By the way, that hat-trick at Twickers was scored against English Schools when Hawker was a member of what he still describes as 'the greatest team I played in'—the unbeaten 1977–78 Australian Schoolboys. The backline of that extraordinary team included the three Ella brothers, Michael O'Connor, Tony Melrose, Dominic Vaughan and Wally Lewis. No wonder they were unbeaten!)

• •

L'Equipe de France

It is easy to make the mistake of assuming that rugby is much the same around the world. Even among those great Five Nations rivals—England, Ireland, Scotland, Wales and France—the game enjoys vastly differing status. In early 1995 I was invited to Europe to do commentary on the Five Nations series for C.S.I. International. A memorable day in France served to prove the contrasts between rugby on the Continent and back home.

MY EXPECTATIONS were that this would be a special adventure. That belief was reinforced at about 3 a.m. on Qantas QF1 as we crossed the Himalayas *en route* to Paris via London. The spectacle outside my cabin window looked like some special effects landscape on a Hollywood set. A seemingly infinite panorama of snow-covered mountains, backlit by an eerie full moon. A sea of needle-point crests, hauntingly beautiful, radiating a magical lunar glow. The captain of the aircraft said he had never seen anything like it in thirty years of flying.

Could this be an omen for Wales, I mused? After all, they hadn't won at Parc des Princes in twenty years.

Paris in January is chilly—6° when I stepped out of Orly

Airport. After establishing contact with Nick Farr-Jones and Ian Borthwick (a freelance rugby journalist based in Paris), lunch was arranged for next day at a stylish restaurant, 'L'Atelier'. Nick and his wife Angie had arrived in Paris just six days earlier to begin a three-year term with Société Générale, France's leading bank. He arrived at the restaurant with his immediate boss, François-Xavier St Macary. François was an old friend from Sydney where he'd had a stint setting up the bank's options trading department. A self-confessed rugby nut, he said he was thrilled to have a man of Nick's calibre on his marketing team. At the same time he pointed out that he was determined to protect Nick from the inevitable barrage of invitations and requests that would flow his way. Australia's winning World Cup captain was taking a new direction in his life and François, a young family man himself, would shield his new protégé. The pair spoke enthusiastically about the first priority—a crash course in French for Monsieur Farr-Jones.

After we'd sampled a tasty *ragoût d'agneau* and a palatable red wine, Ian suggested it was time to depart for French training. Their camp was situated at Château Ricard, 60 kms south-west of Paris in a rural setting of woodlands and lush countryside. The Château, I was told, was a hunting lodge whose master was the revered former French lock, Benoît Dauga. Benoît greeted Ian and myself warmly and then led us into his castle. Inside, we were confronted by a setting of sumptuous comfort—wood-panelled walls, chandeliers and nineteenth-century furniture. Dauga led us to the bar and offered what I presumed would be a hot drink. Ian interpreted for me: a glass of vintage cognac was traditional before training. We accepted, and soon joined a group of journalists and photographers already chatting together in the room.

With what seemed inordinate solemnity we were then informed that the French team would appear at any moment through a door adjacent to the small bar. Coach Pierre Berbizier would apparently also outline his build-up plans for Saturday's big game against defending Five Nations champions, Wales.

Almost on cue *L'Equipe de France* filed out. Benazzi and Roumat, towering figures, brushed politely past. Then Emile N'Tamack, the new wing sensation who'd all but crippled the All Blacks with his blistering intercept try at Eden Park the previous July. (The French won that day after taking the first Test at Christchurch to clinch their first-ever series win on NZ soil). Next out, Philippe Sella. The great man was stern-faced but managed a wink when our eyes met. I felt privileged to be part of this inner sanctum, rubbing shoulders with some of the true stars of international rugby.

Berbizier was last man out and appeared relaxed as as he quietly acknowledged recognisable faces. A walk of 300 metres beside a delightful lake led us to a rugby pitch which was already inhabited by the French 'A' team who were preparing for Scotland 'A' on the weekend. About 1500 spectators, including many school children, chattered excitedly as their idols arrived. This was the same team that had beaten the All Blacks. As the squad did warm-up stretches, young boys stared in awe, so close they could touch their heroes. It was an astonishing turnout for a training session at such an isolated venue. Telephoto lenses continually refocused as the twenty-strong contingent of sports photographers snapped away.

Berbizier is a tiny man, no more than 165 cms. He is France's most capped scrum-half with fifty-six international appearances between 1981–91. The senior team had a two-hour opposed session against the 'A' players (who definitely lifted a few notches given the opportunity to tackle or outrun one of the stars). Berbizier orchestrated match situations and blew his whistle quickly when players took wrong options or were tardy in decision-making.

Towards the end of the session Ian introduced me to Guy Savoy. He owns one of France's leading restaurants, bearing his name, in the heart of Paris. 'What's he doing here?' I enquired. Guy, I was promptly informed, was an enthusiastic rugby man in his thirties who still played the odd social game. He had done his early training as a chef alongside Mark Cecillon, a reserve for Saturday. Along with three other leading French chefs, he had been invited to prepare the evening meal for Quinze France plus reserves. 'What's on the menu?' was my curious follow-up. (For the record, the French national team was served a seven-course meal of the finest French cuisine washed down by the best vintages from the vineyards of Bordeaux and Champagne.)

The temperature dropped to 3° as nightfall set in. The two forward packs then took turns to heave the 'Rhino' scrum machine. Impressive loosehead prop Benezech consulted second rower Merle who was pushing behind him. Merle is a front rower's dream. He tips the scales at 126 kgs and his massive frame and size seventeen boots enable him to push harder than any lock in international rugby. Benezech himself is a lightweight prop and was obviously looking to his somewhat more robust colleague for maximum support in the shove.

With the session finally completed the 'A' team departed by bus while the French squad returned to the château to shower before conducting interviews with the throng of press. Berbizier went straight into the team meeting room and sat down on a stool at the front. It was clearly a familiar procedure. The rugby journalists slowly followed him in while the earlybirds fired a few informal questions.

Berbizier's main thrust was that this was another chapter in a new era and that his revitalised and now disciplined French XV would hopefully pick up where they'd left off in New Zealand. The coach spoke of mental strength and maturity as being key ingredients. He also spoke of the need to provide a spectacle because that was what the public wanted and deserved. In essence, discipline and flair were the hallmarks he was striving to achieve. When those two factors come together in the French XV, they can beat anyone.

Ian and I finally departed Château Ricard at 7 p.m., but not before accepting a parting cognac from our host, Benoît Dauga. Enough said, enough seen. I was convinced there could only be one winner come Saturday—and besides, the moon was only half revealed. In fact, the Tricolores won 21–9 in a fitful display only enlivened by a two-try burst in the middle stages. The match may have been far from memorable, but for me the build-up was unforgettable.

• •

The world wide promotional 'face' of the 1995 World Cup, black winger Chester Williams, almost didn't make it onto the field at all.

Featured on billboards, in print media and on television, Chester was nowhere to be seen when South Africa and Australia kicked off the opening match at Newlands. Due to a hamstring injury he'd been replaced in the Springbok squad.

But, as someone cheekily said after the match against Canada, 'There is a God after all.' An injury to Pieter Hendriks allowed the 80 kilogram winger to gain re-entry into the South African squad.

Williams made sure that he lived up to the World Cup slogan 'The Waiting's Over'. He made a sensational four-try comeback against Western Samoa in the quarter-final which ensured his place in the Cup-winning side at Ellis Park on 24 June.

• •

'Weebollabolla!'

If Wales happen to run onto Cardiff Arms Park for the final of the 1999 World Cup, that curious word may well be their catchcry. It's an Aboriginal word for 'End of the Great Fire', and it also turned out to signify the end of the great drought for the Welsh touring team. After four straight losses, the Scarlets arrived in Moree in June 1996 for the traditional clash with NSW Country. They were hoping for a pleasant interlude in what had so far been a murderous schedule in the 'big smoke'.

Sorry, lads. While Moree's population of 10,000 certainly opened their arms to only the second visit from an international team to the black-soil town in twenty-one years, the fixture at Weebollabolla Oval would not be for the faint-hearted—on either side. The steely band of Welshman certainly hadn't come for the sight-seeing. Their tour was on something of a slippery slide so nothing short of a thumping victory over the NSW Country Cockatoos would be acceptable.

Country coach Paul Murray's pack, led by Cumnock's Andrew McCalman and Gordon 'Chainsaw' Macqueen from Kyogle, was primed and ready to take the Welsh apart. Country's tight-head prop (and former long-haired bikie) Warren Petty was the chief lamb skinner at the Cowra Abbatoirs. He was under orders to employ his dissection skills on the Welsh scrum.

But then came the dawn of Moree's biggest rugby day for a decade and things were begining to look a trifle ominous. After five years of drought, drenching rain had made Weebollabolla Oval into a virtual rice paddy. Welsh conditions.

Country boy 'Chainsaw' felled every Welshman in sight and his team-mates in the pack followed his example with religious fervour. Behind the scrum, former test half Steve Merrick was a standout, showing flashes of the brilliance that took him so briefly to the summit of international rugby last year. But it would all be a lost cause.

Rookie hooker Barry Willimans showed that he'd be more than ready to play in a Wales jumper by the 1999 World Cup, as did young lock Mike Voyle and rising backrower Steve Williams. In the backline the Welsh youngsters grasped their opportunity. Centre Dafydd James and fullback Crispin Cormack overcame the Moree slush to show they were verging on first-team stature.

Wales triumphed 51–3.

Strength from Adversity

The 1981–82 Wallaby tour of Great Britain was a far from impressive expedition for the national team. The results in the Test matches were poor, the squad could have been more unified, and relations between the tour management and some members of the accompanying media deteriorated badly. Yet, in the years to follow, those of us close to Australian rugby saw many of those bitter seeds eventually bear much sweeter fruit.

CARDIFF ARMS PARK was under nearly a metre of snow. The 1981–82 Wallabies had been deprived of one last chance to show their true worth against a star-studded Barbarians line-up. After failing in the tests against Wales, Scotland and England, the lofty aspirations of Bob Templeton's squad had finally been put to rest in an appropriately icy grave.

As a radio reporter and television commentator covering that tour, the cancellation of the Baa-Baa's game was just about the last straw for me. By then I certainly wasn't Tempo's pin-up boy because from the start I'd publicly disagreed with his conservative tactics in the Test matches.

The key man in the prevailing game-plan was fly-half Paul

McLean—for his exercising of backline options and renowned goalkicking. 'Spoofer' was without peer behind a dominant pack. The Queenslander's inspired variation and tactical kicking could demoralise any opposition (as the Waratahs experienced time and again in the second half of the seventies). But on tour, Tempo's preoccupation with McLean came unstuck on two fronts. The 'tight five' just weren't dominant and for some reason goalkicking had become a nightmare for the celebrated Australian No. 10.

I was an unashamed fan of Mark Ella at fly-half and Michael Hawker and Michael O'Connor as his centre partners. Because I'd been filing daily radio reports to the ABC—frequently championing Ella's cause for the Test team—there was no doubt I'd made myself unpopular with some sections of the team. McLean was well aware of my views. I'd been quite happy to discuss the whole issue with him. To accommodate Ella, my proposal was that Paul even shift to inside centre or fullback.

After the solid but unconvincing win over Ireland, manager Sir Nicholas Shehadie called the Australian media into his room when we arrived in Cardiff. Tempo was aware of some of the negative press and I gained the impression that this was to be an exercise in opening more informal lines of communication. Also in attendance were Sinclair Robieson (News Ltd), Ian Telford (AAP), David Lord (freelance) and Frank O'Callaghan (*Courier-Mail*).

We all had our say, although when it came to the crunch I was dismayed at the lack of open support from my colleagues. Of course I'd never expect Frank O'Callaghan— 'Old Maroon Eyes'—to put Mark Ella ahead of Paul McLean, but I was surprised when the remainder of the press party delicately sidestepped the matter.

My personal assessment for the Welsh Test was straightforward. Because the opposition were strong in the 'tight five' Australia would always struggle for parity in the set pieces. We could hope for no more than 40 per cent of possession, at best, and simply couldn't afford to kick the ball away. 'Let's maintain possession and pick a backline that will run at the Welsh. Their midfield players look very suspect in attack and defence,' I pleaded to the gathering. As we left the room Nick thanked me but apparently I'd made little impression. The status quo prevailed.

Those were the days before video analysis and assistant coaches. Tempo was very much on his own. It was down to him and the views of the senior players who, with the exception of John Hipwell, were Queenslanders. Manager Sir Nicholas Shehadie was a wise old head, but perhaps because of his strong Randwick ties he tended to play a diplomatic role. However, my point all along was that the design of Queensland's dominance at provincial level didn't necessarily translate into success in the Test arena against the top nations.

I was certainly a Wallaby critic but—hopefully—an objective and fair one. The parochial interests of NSW or Queensland shouldn't count for anything when it comes to the gold jumper. My radio coverage slowly became something of a crusade against the policies which I believed were undermining Australia's faltering campaign. At Nick Shehadie's request I happily supplied copies of all my radio scripts after each broadcast. Fair enough. When you passionately support a cause you should pursue it—but with eyes and ears open and unafraid of other opinions.

In fairness, Australia would probably have scraped home against Wales if John Hipwell had not been injured in the second half and forced to leave the field. I recall a Welsh supporter saying to me before the previous game, 'Without Hipwell you'd be dead!' He was right. But I'll argue till *my* deathbed that the Wallabies could have won that game comfortably with Ella at fly-half conducting a more adventurous approach.

Then, to compound my frustration, the Aussie brains trust refused to bring on Mark Ella and reshuffle the backline even when Michael Hawker was injured with ten minutes to go.

Instead, Mick Martin was called on as a winger. 'You've got to be kidding,' I fumed to myself while trying to press ahead with a dispassionate television commentary back to Australia. The Wallabies had needed some instant inspiration! At least Mark would have given them a fighting chance.

Despite denials by management there were definitely divisions within that 1981–82 touring team. Perhaps not outwardly, but privately there were many disgruntled players, especially those who couldn't get even the faintest look-in on Test team selection. This is no great revelation, and it was a perfectly understandable situation. But when players are performing well but not getting any substantial recognition it's obviously unhealthy and potentially harmful.

Just one example: did not the NSW pairing of Steve Williams and Mick Mathers warrant serious consideration after their excellent scrummaging and driving play in the loose during the midweek games? Mathers' lack of height was admittedly a liability in the lineouts, but there was no more hungry forward on tour (and the Wallabies struggled at lineout time anyway.) It's worth contrasting the frustrations of that campaign with Greg Smith's approach in Britain in 1996. Only John Eales, Matthew Burke and David Wilson were certain first-team selections. With one or two exceptions, everyone else had a sniff of a Test spot at some stage during the tour. As a consequence the entire squad was firing and morale remained high.

But back on that 1981–82 tour, there was much which seemed to cry out for criticism. Having admired the Alan McGilvray approach in his cricket commentaries since boyhood, I instinctively adopted his outspoken style (although I may have lacked the same level of credibility). I decided it was time to speak out and be prepared to live with the consequences. When Tony Shaw king hit Bill Cuthbertson in the Scottish Test I didn't mince words in my radio wrap-up. 'Tony Shaw should never captain Australia again!'

The script was duly passed on to Sir Nicholas. (Shaw in fact dropped himself for the England Test and as it transpired he had indeed led his country at Test level for the last time.)

That fateful punch was unfortunately the turning point of the game. I regarded Tony Shaw as a mate and still do. It really hurt to make such a public judgment, but I felt it was my duty. Tony has had to live with that spontaneous rush of blood, but happily he's not remembered for that infamous incident. Rather, rugby fans remember him as one of the toughest and most aggressive players ever to pull on an Australian jumper. His crime was that he didn't exercise discretion and wait his moment after being provoked by the grizzly Cuthbertson. We are all guilty of stupid acts in our lives—what a pity Tony's came in front of millions of viewers.

Mark Ella did return to the Test team in that Murrayfield game with McLean shifting to inside centre. Alas, it was too little too late. The 1981–82 Wallabies had lost their way in Britain after being lauded before the tour began as the best Australian squad to leave home shores. Bob Templeton suffered a mild heart attack as the slide set in. Near the end of the tour, David Lord launched a stinging attack on the team's tactics in the national press and also highlighted an alleged split between NSW and Queensland players. It was certainly a stressful tour for the management and a major disappointment for the players.

Yet it wasn't all doom and gloom. There was plenty of sparkling rugby outside the Tests and a host of hilarious moments. When buxom Erica Roe did her famous streak across the hallowed Twickenham turf, England fullback Marcus Rose turned to his skipper Bill Beaumont and suggested, 'Bill, don't look now but there's a lass on the pitch with your buttocks on her chest!'

The Wallabies were based at Porthcawl on the Welsh coastline for the Barbarians match. Although that final game was cancelled because of a heavy snowfall in the south of the country, they still managed to let their hair down. The ever-unpredictable Mick

Martin went for a dip in the icy ocean while some of his team-mates shared a few laughs with the aforementioned Erica Roe, who'd checked into the hotel courtesy of a London tabloid. As it happened she was promptly snowed in for a few days but there were no further confirmed reports of streaking (at least in public).

As often happens towards the end of any tour, discussion began turning to the future. ARU powerbroker and former Wallaby, Ross Turnbull, asked my opinion on who should take over as national coach. 'Easy,' I replied, 'Bob Dwyer. He's a coach committed to fifteen-man rugby. We've got the backs—let's use them.' I claim no Nostradamus-like powers; you didn't have to be Einstein to make that suggestion. Turnbull soon became Dwyer's staunchest ally and was instrumental in the change of national coach the following season. Nevertheless, two years later the same man—Turnbull—helped depose Dwyer and steer Alan Jones into the same job after the Wallabies had failed in France.

With all roads in Cardiff closed, my enduring memory at the end of the 1981–82 Wallaby tour is driving along the railway line in a four-wheel drive vehicle with former Wallaby, Peter Crittle, and a few of his lawyer mates. It was the only way out of the snowbound city. 'Charlie' Crittle came out with a profound statement as we ploughed nervously through the snow: 'It's time the Australian team had two coaches—one for the backs and one for the forwards'. Alan Jones successfully utilised Alec Evans as a forward coach from 1984 onwards.

And there was no more delighted media man than myself in 1988 when Bob Dwyer began his second term as national coach and promptly appointed Bob Templeton as his lieutenant. Although I'd disagreed with Tempo in the early eighties, I always respected him. It was a special joy to watch his partnership with Dwyer mould our greatest rugby triumph—the World Cup victory at Twickenham in late 1991.

Munster Mayhem

Visiting teams have had the temerity to suggest that if you strapped a pillow to each corner post, the ground could double as a boxing ring. Thomond Park in Limerick is the real nerve centre of Irish rugby. Also known as the 'Gardens of Get Somebody' and 'The Killing Fields', the sacred turf at headquarters is renowned for some famous Munster conquests.

'KICK AHEAD! Kick a head! Kick *any* head!'

That famous catch cry of the Men From Munster has echoed through decades of fiercely contested rugby confrontation with wary touring teams.

The 'boots-and-all' approach of the local players is legendary. Munster is old Viking territory—the Danes settled in the area in the eleventh century. Then, in the seventeenth century, William of Orange won a long battle against the Jacobites who'd bravely defended their city. But the subsequent Treaty of Limerick was broken by the English—which led to generations of bitterness and rebellion.

Yes, they're proud, parochial people down Munster way and you'd swear that legacy has spilt over into the sporting arena.

Rugby is religion in the Deep South of Ireland. Indeed, there's a school of thought that Ireland would often be better served if the entire Munster squad swapped their scarlet jerseys for the emerald green of the national team.

Two Wallaby sides have had their noses rubbed into Thomond Park's fertile soil, but the most famous victory of all for the home team will always be their shock 12–0 triumph over the 1978 Grand Slam-winning All Blacks. Fly-half Tony Ward kicked the two most important drop goals of his colourful career on that memorable afternoon, while flanker Christy Cantillon's try—the lone touchdown of the game—is still more famous in the Ring of Kerry than Gordon Hamilton's epic effort in the 1991 World Cup quarter-final against Australia at Lansdowne Road. Munster has run the Springboks perilously close on several occasions but is yet to lower the South African colours. Two of the three fixtures produced margins of just five and six points.

Home wins against international oppposition at Thomond Park are so treasured they acquire potent commercial value. Match programs for the 1978 All Black game were sold out an hour before kick-off and reprinted in large quantities a day *later* to meet the insatiable demand for souvenirs! That 20p program is worth at least fifty pounds today. In 1992, the Bank of Ireland printed a special poster to commemorate Munster's inspired victory that year over Bob Dwyer's Wallabies. This, too, quickly became collectors' items.

But occasionally the Munstermen have come off second best. Take the 1984 clash against the Alan Jones-coached Wallabies. Folklore has it that Munster's number-one game plan is always to kick high. If that fails, Plan B is to kick even higher. The Irish call it 'the art of swarming'—if you put the ball up high enough it gives the lads a bit of time to think.

For the 1984 game Thomond Park was engulfed in a pea-soup fog. The Wallabies were on their way to a Grand Slam and in no mood to treat the midweek game lightly. After assessing the conditions Alan Jones devised a crafty bit of reverse psychology. Enter one Roger Gould, the biggest punt kicker in the game. With visibility down to just twenty metres, 'Big Rog' was instructed to unleash a fusillade of his booming big berthas. Munstermen could be faintly observed through the fog running around in panic-stricken circles as gold jumpers charged through enemy lines in attack formation. The Wallabies couldn't actually see the falling ball, but knew Gould's kicking well enough to anticipate its flight path. The carefully devised tactics created the desired havoc and the result was never in doubt. It was an eerie experience to watch from the grandstand: you'd hear the sound of Gould's thundering boot on leather—and then had to wait for the shrill pitch of the referee's whistle to indicate a try had been scored.

Greg Smith's unbeaten 1996 Wallabies to Britain and Ireland adopted very different tactics for their wintry afternoon visit to Thomond Park. Even two weeks out from the game the non-Test players were talking about the looming midweek clash and the level of ferocity and intensity needed to quell the local challenge. Assistant coach Jake Howard had stated from the start of the tour that Munster would be the Wallabies' fifth Test match.

Arriving at the ground on that grey Tuesday afternoon, one quickly gained the impression from the Limerick locals that prospects were bleak for the Australians. There were no fewer than nine internationals in the Munster side, all blazing with passion and joyfully anticipating the massacre of yet another famous touring side. In the visitors' dressing room our players were like caged lions. It was their last chance to press claims for the Test clash with Wales the following Sunday. Additionally, it would be the last match on tour for many of the squad because there was no midweek game before the campaign finale against the Barbarians.

The pre-match psyche-up noises emanating from the Aussie shed were, quite frankly, scary. I remember double-checking with tour manager Peter Falk whether there had been a mix-up in the change rooms. The shouts and screams sounded like feeding time at the zoo. Any moment I expected our golden gladiators to burst through the brick wall and straight onto the field.

Outside, just as in 1978, the crowd were hanging from the rafters. I bumped into Chris Handy and members of his supporters' group who expressed concern that there was no kicker named in the Wallaby backline. With the benefit of my visit to the players' tunnel I was immediately able to allay their fears. 'Don't worry, we won't need one!'

And we didn't: 55–19 to the Wallabies, nine tries to one. It was the worst defeat in Munster's proud history, and arguably the greatest performance of any Wallaby midweek side. The Australian forward pack was on fire, striking straight up centre field at Munster's heart and then unleashing the eager backs. It was breathtaking stuff.

Inspiring ACT Brumbies' skipper Brett Robinson assumed the role of General Custer while Tim Gavin, David Giffin and Owen Finegan threw themselves into the fray with awesome power and commitment. They were clearly posing the selectors the big question: 'Why aren't we in the Test team?' All three forwards finished up playing against Wales five days later; indeed every Wallaby player on Thomond Park demonstrated impressive Test match qualifications. David Campese produced his best game of the tour while fly-half Pat Howard cleverly underplayed his hand, focusing on passing and supporting with just an occasional chip or grubber. Those performances earned the third-generation Wallaby and Campo their Test recalls.

The game was also the turning point for the Greg Smith regime. After sustained criticism from reporters on tour and critics back home, this was a long-overdue victory—with style. It combined forward smash-and-grab with exciting backline panache—the desired Smith recipe. Up until the Munster match we'd seen the ingredients but never the finished product.

The local Limerick crowd took the loss extremely well. Once they realised their heroes' cause was hopeless, their response to Australia's wizardry became not just appreciative but enthusiastic. After the game the Wallabies were mobbed by the admiring locals. It was a truly memorable day of rugby.

Significantly, Australia's prospects of completing their tour unbeaten were never in doubt from that moment. The true will and character of the Wallaby squad had at last spoken. History will record that performance as one of the most outstanding fifteen-man displays of running rugby ever turned on by an Australian touring team.

In 1987 the individual world record for most points in an International was broken twice in the same day.

Gavin Hastings scored twenty-seven points at Dunedin in Scotland's crushing 55–28 victory over Romania. Just an hour later in Auckland, France rattled up seventy points to down Zimbabwe.

Fullback Didier Camberabera scored three tries and kicked nine conversions for an amazing personal total of thirty points. And bear in mind that was under the old scoring system!

• •

If international referee Tony Spreadbury needs to raise his voice, take good heed. His is a voice of considerable authority.

A few years back Spreadbury was officiating in an otherwise uneventful Scottish inter-district match between Edinburgh and Melrose.

Without permission, a Jack Russell hunting dog suddenly scampered onto the field and exhibited every intention of joining in the play.

But the hapless hound hadn't reckoned on Mr Spreadbury.

The ref immediately unleashed a shrill blast from his whistle, gestured violently toward the grandstand and bellowed 'Off you! Right now!'

Shortly afterwards, footage of the incident was replayed in the 'What Happened Next?' segment of the popular BBC television quiz show *A Question of Sport*.

The picture was frozen just as the dog gazed up at the referee. The best the bemused contestants could come up with as to what happened next was that perhaps the canine had paused to answer a call of nature.

They'd underestimated the authority of Tony Spreadbury.

In fact, the dog had been so overawed by the referee's imperious command to take an early shower that it immediately turned and slunk out through the gate—straight into the Visitors' change room.

• •

Please, Sir

It's not the done thing to fire too many critical broadsides at poor old 'Sir', but prompted by an absolutely atrocious display the previous week from another UK whistle-blower, I used my weekly column in Sydney's Daily Telegraph *to submit this 'Memorandum' to the next Tri-Nations referee.*

MEMO: Mr James Fleming of Scotland
                 (Referee)
SUBJECT: Australia v New Zealand
DATE: 27th July, 1996
PLACE: Suncorp Stadium

Sir,

With the utmost respect, we assume you have noted the dramatic changes that are transforming the game down here in our part of the world of late.

The players have adopted a tremendously positive attitude. So too, I'm delighted to report, have the referees.

As a result the code has enjoyed a spectacular upsurge in popularity. Through sensible man-management by the referees, the players have been able to express their great talents for the enjoyment of all concerned.

In this light, I must raise the rather disconcerting performance of your countryman, Mr Ray Megson, in last Saturday's Test at Lancaster Park.

We fully understand that Mr Megson is very proud of his brand new whistle, but he is yet to embrace our style of refereeing. Assisted (some might even say 'aided and abetted') by the frequent on-field interruptions of your third panel member, Mr Ken McCartney, he managed to blow an impressive total of no fewer than thirty-seven free kicks and penalties during the game.

I concede that the assembled multitudes were left in no doubt that Mr Megson's whistle is in splendid working order.

Indeed, I have no particular objection to the penalties as such. However, I appeal to you—one of the world's premier referees—to at least give consideration to our new and outstandingly successful approach.

The key words are 'positive' and 'attitude'. They are not terribly difficult to remember.

The rugby public, at the ground and watching on television, have no particular wish to witness forty penalties per match. Nor do the players. Perhaps it is a reflection of our colonial past, but we don't believe it is necessary for the referee to report *every single offence*.

In our humble submission, the arbiter's prime obligation is to ensure that the right people get the right ball.

The fundamentals of applying this simple principle depend on a firm understanding of the breakdown where the tackle or stoppage occurs.

To this end, your brother referees in the Antipodes have

agreed a general set of operational procedures (which follow herewith):

* Make your decision early in each tackle.
* Don't wait to see if people are going to fall over.
* Determine if the delivery path or 'birth canal' of the ball is clear.
* If it is, then virtually anything goes.
* Allow the ball to emerge, and talk people away who are trying to prevent its release.
* But, if the ball is 'killed' by an illegality, then penalise early, within the first three or four seconds of the tackle.
* If, on the other hand, you decide that the ball is available, spend the next few seconds talking people out of infringements. This style of 'preventative refereeing' is preferable to whistle-blowing.
* Set these ground rules early in the match by penalising initial offenders who stifle continuity.

It is our considered opinion that the adoption of these principles—as demonstrated by Ed Morrison and Wayne Erickson in recent Internationals—provides a far superior spectacle by yielding only half the number of penalties.

We trust you will have an enjoyable game.

Yours respectfully,

GORDON BRAY

Wilfred Wooler was still a schoolboy when he played for Wales in their historic first win at Twickenham.

Wooler remains one of the most remarkable figures in Welsh sport. He was capped eighteen times as a winger and centre before World War II, and in 1939 even managed to squeeze in a stint in soccer as centre-forward for Cardiff City.

A Cambridge Blue in rugby and cricket, he was lucky to survive the war after being taken prisoner in 1941 by the Japanese in Java.

When peace returned, Wooler made over 400 appearances for Glamorgan Country Cricket Club, scoring more than 12,000 runs and capturing nearly 900 wickets over fourteen seasons. In the 1950s he was an England cricket selector and even found time to represent Wales at squash.

A generation later, the great star of Welsh rugby was their fullback and occasional flanker, J.P.R. Williams.

Yet the man who played so well against Australia in 1978 had also been a tennis player of considerable ability. Just ask England's former No.1 and Davis Cup player David Lloyd.

In 1966, Lloyd lost to the young JPR in the junior Wimbledon singles title. Williams then gave his tennis racquet a rest while accumulating sixty-three caps for Wales and the Lions over thirteen seasons.

He is now a prominent orthopaedic surgeon.

French Follies

When visiting national rugby teams tour their territory, the French administrators take delight in producing exhausting itineraries that criss cross the country. Many of the hotels they choose are strategically placed in the middle of nowhere. During the Wallaby tour of 1976, this led to a life-and-death experience.

THE MOST MEMORABLE venue of the 1976 tour was Perigeux, in Dordogne, where the Wallabies were scheduled to take on one of those notorious *Selections Français*. The team's base was decidedly rural, about 25 kms out of town. After a quick reconnaissance of the surrounding district, the Wallaby scouting party stumbled upon a medieval castle which turned out to be a German-style beer house. After negotiating the 'drawbridge' (a partly submerged weir) we met the hostess who promptly invited the entire touring party to a beer festival she was holding that night.

To a man, the gallant Wallabies accepted the invitation. For visitors in a foreign land to do otherwise would, surely, have been churlish. Australian rugby's finest then proceeded to prove the legendary proportions of their thirsts. Late into the night I recall two of the front rowers, Ronnie Graham and Steve Finnane, engaged in earnest conversation with a caged monkey. The beer kept flowing and a memorable time was had by all.

But all good things must also come to an end. At 2.30 a.m. the Australian manager, John Bain—a former Wallaby hooker of appropriate bulk—suggested I should show him the way back to the team hotel. Realising that the whole future of the tour was now in my hands, I led the way out to the weir. To my dismay we discovered that our path home was now submerged by a fast-moving torrent due to heavy rain. Many of the Wallabies had already decided to sleep in the castle because the current was too dangerous.

Nevertheless (at least in my happy, befuddled mind), the well-being of Australian rugby depended on its tour manager regaining the safety of the team hotel. Because John was no longer in a state to negotiate the crossing under his own steam, I offered to piggy back him across. He pinched a beach umbrella to keep us dry (subsequently returned by the duty boy next day), and off we waded, my seventy kilos supporting his 110. Only a rush of Dutch courage carried me across.

In hindsight, my only closer 'brush with death' was during the gale-torn Sydney–Hobart Race in 1984. To this day, manager Bain denies the incident ever occurred. A generous man might say he couldn't *remember* it.

As tour managers went, John Bain made a very good selector, and I say that with all sincerity. By his own admission he'd been given the job in France for 'services rendered'. John would also agree that he simply wasn't ready to be thrown in at the deep end, mothering a squad of twenty-six young men—the majority on their first trip to a non-English-speaking country.

But 'Bainey' had his own special skills, and the former Wallaby hooker of the fifties was in scintillating form after the first Test loss in Bordeaux. With midnight a distant memory and the hotel bar firmly closed John suddenly became 'The World's Greatest Manager' as far as myself and a group of Wallabies were concerned. He accepted our challenge to sneak behind the bar and serve us a few more drinks. There was absolutely no impropriety—the money was left on the bar. We just needed some additional 'settlers' to help soothe the trauma of a three-point defeat at the hands of the French XV.

Regrettably, the hotel management didn't quite see it that way. The terrifying, two-note blare of a *gendarme* siren was soon hurtling towards us through the early morning silence. Players, media and manager scattered in all directions and an international incident was thereby avoided (but not before we all experienced that special adrenalin rush which comes from being 'wanted by the police').

The episode came to a hilarious conclusion next morning. Manager Bain called all players and media to his room for a team meeting. The solemn look on his face gave those in the know an inkling of what was to follow.

'Gentlemen! It's been brought to my attention by the hotel management that a member of our team was pouring drinks last night when the bar was closed. That sort of behaviour just can't be tolerated. I'll be making strenuous enquiries and if the claims are correct then that player will be on the first plane home!' (Sounds of stifled laughter mixed with the groans of the severely hung over.)

John Bain was a man of his word, but fortunately the claims were never substantiated and no culprit was found. Perhaps he had simply exercised his rights under British law and declined to come forward with certain evidence on the grounds that it might incriminate him . . . ?

Trevor Allan's 1949 Wallabies were the first Australian team to win the Bledisloe Cup on New Zealand soil, taking the first test 11–6 at Wellington and the second at Eden Park by 16–9. It was a side which boasted some great names.

Stars in the forward pack included second-rowers Nick Shehadie (later Lord Mayor of Sydney and Chairman of SBS televison), and a 21-year-old debutant called Rex Mossop. 'The Moose' always wore his sleeves rolled up well past the elbow to send a symbolic message to his opponents that he intended getting amongst the hard work. Another to pack down for his first test alongside Mossop at Wellington was a young breakaway named Dave Brockhoff, later to become Wallaby coach. Apart from skipper Allan, the standout in the backs that afternoon was yet another newcomer, the dashing 21-year old winger from Sydney University, Ralph Garner. Garner, who'd learned his rugby at Armidale, crossed for two sparkling tries but retired from representative rugby after the 1949 tour to concentrate on his medical studies.

But according to Brockhoff, that historic win at Athletic Park was driven more by fear than playing ability. Manager for the tour was big Ron Walden, a senior officer in the Sydney Vice Squad and a man of 'forceful character'. The coach was 'Wild Bill' Cerutti, another daunting figure who'd earned his legendary status as an uncompromising forward before the War. That pair could strike fear into any heart.

Brockhoff remembers a touch-and-go incident just before the tour. 'Walden caught me gambling on flight night at the old Sydney Stadium and said he wouldn't take me to New Zealand if I didn't give up the habit,' he told me. As a management team they were so different. Bill with his wild antics—he used to eat the flowers off the table at dinner—and Ron with his tough policeman attitude. They were revered by the players, but it was a reign of terror.'

The Jones Era

Love him or hate him, Alan Jones has an amazing ability to attract attention and get his message across. As Wallaby coach in the mid-80s he cut an unforgettable swathe through British rugby. Two years later, in the Land of the Long White Cloud, he broke all the rules on the way to an epic series win over the All Blacks—only the fourth time a touring team had downed the Kiwis and the first a Wallaby outfit had taken a three-Test series from New Zealand on their home turf. The Jones style defined a whole era of Australian rugby.

IN BRITAIN in 1984, Alan Jones' single-minded thirst for the Grand Slam and a place in sporting history set the tone for the whole campaign. After suffering the indignity of a 2–1 series loss to the All Blacks, (the decider at the SCG had been a 25–24 heartbreaker) Jones gave Mark Ella his head in the UK and the Aussie backs ran riot. But Jones only 'threw the switch to vaudeville' after he'd carefully beefed up his forwards with lineout giants and a massive front row. The underlying strategy was simple: win as much ball as possible, recycle it quickly and above everything—retain it. It worked like a charm.

That equation wasn't employed in such a straightforward form in New Zealand in 1986. For starters, there was no longer a Mark Ella to weave his attacking magic—he'd surprisingly retired after the Grand Slam tour. The Kiwi opposition presented a far more intimidating challenge. Jones very quickly constructed a deliberately provocative 'us and them' team mentality. In public he made enemies at every turn, yet still found time to deliver statesmanlike addresses to a sprinkling of favoured rugby clubs along the way. He upset the New Zealand hierarchy with his outspoken comments and even publicly called one official a 'turd'. He criticised team accommodation and even led a lock-stock-and-barrel walkout of a hotel in Thames—with every justification, I might add.

Jones was under enormous pressure and didn't always keep his temper in check. None who witnessed it could ever forget his unmerciful tongue lashing of a TVNZ crew who were spotted filming an Australian training session without permission. It was vintage Alan Jones, and deserved an Oscar nomination at least. He stopped the session and stormed off towards the intruders. The withering verbal barrage seemed to last at least five minutes. Just when he appeared to be ending his tirade, both barrels were quickly reloaded for another high calibre blast. Naturally, the camera kept rolling and the incident was headlined on the TV news service that night. Yet amid all this off-field melodrama, the Wallabies themselves managed to tip toe through the minefield (some would say created by their coach) and triumphed in the deciding third Test at Eden Park by 22–9.

To some, the New Zealand series win was a finer achievement than the 1984 tour of the United Kingdom by the Eighth Wallabies, but it is that Grand Slam which still defines the Jones era. With some justification that team has been hailed as our greatest ever, although the arguments will continue on that subject as long as beer flows across a rugby club bar. They travelled the length and breadth of Britain and Ireland playing the running game. The accent was on fitness and commitment, and those essential skills of passing, handling and supporting—all executed with a high degree of athleticism. The 1984 tour was a piece of instant rugby history, and as a reporter travelling with the team I made sure to collect some quotes which would help preserve their triumph for posterity.

The chairman of the British Sports Council, Dickie Jeeps, a scrum-half who won more caps for his country and the Lions than any other England player, was impressed by the sheer exhilaration of the Wallabies' style.

DICKIE JEEPS: Having seen this present bunch of Australian players I've been thrilled to bits because they've expanded the game. We play a very negative game over here in the British Isles and they've shown us if you support the ball and run with it you create overlaps. All they've really done is run overlaps. They've run around the outside of the man with possession of the ball. Like your Australian rugby league side, they came here a few years back and showed us our game was out of date. I also believe this Wallaby team has addressed past deficiencies. This time they've got a good scrum, they got a lot more ball in the lineout than expected and they haven't half used that ball tremendously well.

Ian Robertson, a former Scottish fly-half and three-quarter, applauded the Australian fifteen man approach.

IAN ROBERTSON: I'm a great fan of Roger Gould. I think that he has given the sort of solidity at fullback that makes it easier for people to take chances in front of him. Because if things go wrong, they know they've got the 'Rock of Gibraltar' standing there ready to tidy up if necessary. I've loved all the back play, and all the clever quick handling as they're able to use their wrists to flip the ball along. They also run straight. They have centres running parallel to the touchline and then creating space for the rest of the backs.

So that's a team involvement, but individually I've loved watching Campese. I think he's a smashing player. I've loved the way Mark Ella has orchestrated it throughout the tour, not as a great deep thinker of the game but instinctively—doing the right thing and calling the right shots. I thought the centres both played their part in the team framework but I have to say the scrum-half, Nick Farr-Jones, has had a marvellous tour. What a discovery he's been.

It's been a breath of fresh air watching Australia play rugby over here and it's been a salutary lesson to us and we salute you for what you've taught us. Each player has contributed in his own way. You've had forceful strong wings, Ian Williams has shown magical little touches coming over late in the tour. I'd hate to think how many marvellous players you've got hidden in the outback of Australia. Everybody who's come over as a replacement has played well. Greg Burrow had a great tour when he arrived.

And of course your forwards can all run and handle. I loved the back row—Cody's also had a smashing tour, Tuynman has been a revelation. He's up there with the great All Black number eights like Mexted. He's in that sort of framework as a footballer. But unlike previous Australian packs they do the 'donkey work' as well. Their scrum has improved, they've worked hard at it and they're now a very good scrummaging side. But thankfully they use that as a means to give the ball to the backs, not as Pontypool do, a means to bore us all to death.

One of the outstanding games was the International at Cardiff Arms Park which produced a record 28–9 victory for the Australians. For massive hooker Tommy Lawton, it was an occasion he'll always cherish. His late grandfather had played on the same ground nearly sixty years earlier. Suddenly, there he was crossing the Welsh goal-line for Australia's first try.

TOMMY LAWTON: Yeah, I got tackled and found myself falling over the line. When the referee blew his whistle I thought it must have been a penalty. I got up, his hand was in the air, he was smiling, I was smiling. It was just fantastic. It's the first try I've scored since I was twelve, I think. I really think it all started with our scrum. We attacked them and when Stephens hit the turf with a rib injury we knew they were gone. We hurt them in the scrum and then to score the pushover try, well, that was something you dream about.

Perhaps the most magical aspect of the 1984 tour was that it contained a unique personal Grand Slam within the team's great performances. The incomparable Mark Ella scored a try in every test.

MARK ELLA: We stated that we wanted to play attractive rugby and that we thought we could do it in the four Test matches. We certainly achieved that goal and personally I'm thrilled to be going back home both victorious and scoring a try in each of the four Internationals. The 1977–78 Schoolboys played that type of rugby. Also as Michael Lynagh, Steve Tuynman and Matthew Burke came through on the 1981–82 Schoolboys' tour, it emphasised that we're learning at a very early age to play open, attacking football. With all of those guys coming through I feel there is a great tie-up with this Wallaby side.

More than any other factor, it was the work of the Australian forwards that ensured the success of the tour. Scottish prop Ian Milne, then rated the best tighthead in Britain, gave them high praise.

IAN MILNE: I think one of the major reasons for your success was the solidity up-front. It gave you a platform to work and move all the skills you've always had. Not only was it the scrum and lineout but you were also very strong with any loose ball on the deck. You won a lot of possession there. In the lineout you had the advantage of three very good jumpers—one which none of the four Home countries enjoyed. Having a huge hooker like Lawton put a lot of pressure on the opposition scrum. Especially when he had two solid props as well. I think McIntyre has been a bit of an unsung hero. Rodriguez has had a lot of praise but McIntyre scrummaged very well.

Another crucial ingredient in the 1984 success was the leadership of Andy Slack. Sadly, his immense qualities in this sphere were only discovered in the twilight of his career, but he confounded many doubters before the tour.

ANDREW SLACK: I'm sure people were sceptical but I don't think any national sporting team goes away without high ambition. That's the way sportsmen are. We had a bit of knowledge when we started out because we knew what we were capable of, and what we expected came true. Naturally I'm pleased it did, not only for our satisfaction but also for the people in Britain and Ireland to realise that we are a rugby nation.

But above any individual achievement, the driving force behind the Australian team was coach Alan Jones. A perfectionist and disciplinarian, Jones earned the respect of his team and the opposition. His meticulous preparation for every game always had the Wallabies on the front foot. True, his era was never short on colour or controversy, but it yielded results.

His deputy Alec Evans provided magnificent technical support for the forwards. Alec also assisted Greg Smith's successful 1996 Wallabies. He is definitely one of Australian rugby's unsung heroes.

Jones went on to leave the Wallaby coaching job in controversial circumstances and switch to rugby league where he found limited success. Today he's one of the top talk-back radio hosts in the country, and every now and then some hapless listener is treated to the type of 'spray' he once handed out to that NZ television crew more than a decade ago.

* *

Australia has a proud tradition of producing brilliant scrum-halves, and for many, Ken Catchpole remains the greatest of them all.

But can we remember how his illustrious career came to its premature end?

It was the twenty-fourth minute of the second half of the first Test in 1968 against New Zealand at the SCG. With Australia trailing 19–3, Catchpole was dragged by one leg from a ruck by Colin Meads, suffering a horrific groin injury.

A then new ruling by the IRB permitted replacements for injured players, and at that moment, as one magnificent Test career was ending, another began.

Twenty-year-old John Hipwell came on to replace Catchpole. It would be the first of his splendid thirty-five caps.

* *

Rugby's glorious history is rich with the exploits of talented athletes who've excelled in other areas than their ability with the leather football.

England's Cyril 'Kit' Lowe was capped twenty-five times as a winger in the early years of this century. He was also a representative-level player in cricket, athletics, swimming and boxing. At just 168 cms and 54 kgs, Lowe's critics claimed he was simply too small for the rigours of international rugby. He promptly answered those doubters with eight Test tries in a single season. The valour of his rugby transferred to warfare. As a fighter pilot during World War I he claimed thirty-one enemy aircraft shot down.

During that same era, the Irish centre James Parke played seven seasons of international rugby before hanging up his boots to concentrate on tennis.

While the Wallabies were winning their 1908 Olympic rugby gold medal in London, Parke was across town collecting a silver medal for the men's doubles.

Four years later, Parke had the temerity to sail out here and win the Australian singles title.

But, for sheer excellence in an incredible number of sports, it's hard to imagine anyone surpassing our own Reginald 'Snowy' Baker. In 1904, Snowy was capped twice at scrum-half against the touring British team. He also represented Australia in boxing, polo, swimming and diving, as well as competing in top-level rowing, wrestling, surfing and equestrian events.

Before graduating to a career as a silent-film star, Baker fought for the middleweight boxing gold medal at the 1908 Olympics. His opponent was the future England cricket captain J.W.H.T. Douglas.

The crowd agreed Snowy had won that bout fair-and-square, but Baker lost the gold medal on points. The 'man in the middle' (who'd scored the fight) just happened to be . . . Douglas's father!

Tartan Triumph

It has been my good fortune to witness, first hand, some of the most emotional moments in modern international rugby. My job often also involves reporting the build-up to many of these events. That extra perspective helps cement them in my memory, none more vivid than Scotland's victory over France in Paris during the 1995 Five Nations series.

THE SUN was just poking through as we drove up the Champs Elysée in our Mercedes limousine. I'd hitched a ride with the BBC and we were bound for Maison Lafitte, site of Scottish training on the eve of match day. My companion in the back seat was the 'voice of international rugby', the doyen himself, Bill McLaren. 'You know, son,' he said, 'the only time I've ever screeched was at Stade Colombes in 1969. That was the occasion of Scotland's last Five Nations win in Paris. It was a narrow squeak by 6–3. We'd been hopelessly outplayed, the French had bombed a cluster of tries. But when Jim Telfer charged across from three yards out I was a wee bit jumpy in the box.'

Even Bill had an air of resignation about the pending clash

against France at Parc des Princes. After all, the Scots had gone nine matches without a win before arresting the slump with a win over disappointing Canada a month earlier, followed by victory over Ireland after coming from behind. There would no doubt be a strong French recovery, too, after their recent dismemberment at Twickenham. I wasn't so sure. Two days earlier the French coach, Pierre Berbizier, had conducted a packed press conference for the French rugby media highlighting, by way of an edited video, where the match had been lost against the English. With the sound turned down, the frustrated French coach described the twenty-six times France lost possession in the match. Three days before the Scottish clash he was still brooding about the end of their Grand Slam aspirations! As an outsider I found it strange that he should take this course of action. Why was it necessary to highlight the team's mistakes to the French media? (After all, they had seen the game for themselves.)

Berbizier summarised that it wasn't a case of England being so good but more a case of L'Equipe de France being so inept. The French players had seen the same tape three hours earlier. They were shouldering the blame, but to my mind the coach must surely also share some responsible for faulty technique when it is so widespread. Chinks were appearing in the French armour. With the unmistakable undercurrent that French aspirations were now switching towards the World Cup, the Scots could surely 'go for broke'. And they did.

As their final practice session of thirty-five minutes wound up, Bill McLaren muttered in his rich Scottish brogue, 'Uuuh Gawrrdon, the French and Scottish sessions were like chalk and cheese. These boys dropped the ball three times in the first ten minutes. The French nay spilt that many in an hour and a half.' True enough I thought, but which side would have its eye on the ball next day?

A horde of Scottish journalists attended the session as well as about 500 locals, plus a handful of kilted Scottish supporters. They all swarmed onto the field after the warm down—led, of course, by the kids. The players were scattered across the field signing autographs and doing spot interviews. The whole thing seemed to be quite impromptu. If it wasn't planned, then the Scottish management of Doug Morgan and Duncan Patterson had produced a public relations masterstroke. I wandered from player to player and caught the end of a television interview with Scottish and Lions' captain Gavin Hastings. He reckoned it was about time his team stormed the citadel at Parc Des Princes. 'All losing runs have to end, so why not now?' he said.

I introduced myself to open-side flanker Ian Morrison. Our conversation revealed a fascinating character who professionally was the Director of Bond Sales for the Swiss Bank Corporation in London. I specifically wanted to find out more about his unusual hobby of collecting antique glasses. 'At the start of the season you fill out a form which includes listing your hobbies. I couldn't very well write down "drinking pints and shagging lassies" so I put down "collecting antique glasses".'

'Is it genuine?' I enquired. 'Oh yes. I've got about forty-eight beer and wine glasses dating back to the 1880s and they're all in constant use!' At thirty-two years of age you'd be excused for thinking Morrison's best rugby days were behind him. He had broken both legs playing the game, and carried a steel plate and ten screws in the right one. Yet next day he hunted and harassed with all the resolve of a Scotch terrier.

As I strolled past another little group of players and admirers, a voice called out after me. 'If you get a chance Gordon, send my regards to Blondo and the boys at Eastern Suburbs.' The voice belonged to Craig Joiner, the right winger who'd spent the 1993 season with Easts' first grade colts in Sydney under coach John Blondin.

The Scotland No. 8, Eric Peters, was quieter than many of his team mates. He'd captained Cambridge University to their win over Oxford in 1992, but was also the butt of a common joke I'd heard from several Englishmen on the tour. 'He's only in the Bath second XV, you know,' they scoffed. To put that into its true perspective, Bath's first XV contained no fewer than fifteen capped Internationals. Eric was forced to rotate with John Hall, Andy Robinson, Ben Clarke and Steve Ojomoh.

Peters sports a crew cut and has lost a front tooth (one presumes from one of his regular training sessions with the then world heavyweight boxing champion, Frank Bruno). I was also fascinated to learn that he didn't take up rugby until he was sixteen because he attended a soccer school in Essex. He began his first season of rugby in the centres but soon realised he was taller than all the forwards.

Melrose scrum-half Bryan Redpath was leaning quietly against the pavilion wall, boots in hand, waiting for team mates. I popped a question that had been intriguing me for months. 'Bryan, I understand you have two rugby playing brothers. Did you all play together in the first XV at Melrose?' A broad smile preceded his reply. 'Yeah, we did. One, though, has just had knee surgery and the other is a long-distance lorry driver, so it's a bit difficult for him to play.' Bryan had been criticised for his indecisive play in Scotland's recent Internationals. His relaxed frame of mind on match eve however, proved to be a telling omen.

Meanwhile, for a rugby trivia buff such as myself the Scots turned out to be a delight. Back rower Rob Wainwright, like his father, had won a Cambridge rugby blue. Centre Ian Jardine's four brothers had all played with him at Stirling County. With a canny mixture of premonition and hope, the entire team had placed bets of a 'fiver' per man with a French bookmaker at the staggering odds of 80–1. Would I be able to resist the temptation of including that interesting tidbit in the television call next day?

The match started at frantic pace before a packed house and

the French scored the opening try after just two and a half minutes. But a bout of Gallic over-confidence saw them soon 'blow' two more five-point opportunities in the early stages. Meanwhile, a playing season with the Warringah Green Rats in Sydney had clearly done no harm to the flair and vision of Scotland's outside centre Gregor Townsend. He picked up an opportunist try to help his side to a 10–5 half-time lead. As the five-minute break concluded, I overheard Gavin Hastings' closing words from the Scottish huddle in my earphones: 'Get back and support, lads, and take them on every time'.

Nevertheless, France clawed back in the second half to establish a 21–16 lead with time almost up. But Hastings' fighting half-time words would ultimately win the day. A gallant final 'Highland fling' saw Townsend take on the French defence just outside the twenty-two. Hastings screamed up on the inside as he veered onto the ball and took the surprising one-handed reverse flick. The defence parted like the Red Sea and the conversion gave Scotland an improbable victory which left the celebrated French team in tatters. Scotland's first win at the Parc des Princes and the first in Paris since Bill McLaren's famous screech some twenty-six years earlier!

Emotion poured from the jubilant Scots as their excited coach Dougie Morgan ran onto the pitch. Long after the players had disappeared into their dressing room the Scottish supporters continued to rejoice in the stands behind both goalposts. A full pipe band suddenly materialised and marched onto the arena, playing with gusto and precision. Surely a first at the famous ground. The skirl of the pipes acted like a siren's call to the Scottish fans who'd already left the arena. They swarmed back through the exits and into the Parc.

The triumphant Scottish players, now barefooted and some wearing French jumpers, answered the call of their countrymen and sprinted back onto the pitch. First they ran to the northern end where the ecstatic supporters sang 'Flower of Scotland', all the while being conducted by their heroes. The players then jogged down to the southern end and repeated the ritual. When they finally began returning to the dressing rooms they were given a standing ovation. None stood more proudly than Bill McLaren and his co-commentator John Jeffrey in the BBC box. Even the Princess Royal, attending the match as patron of the Scottish Rugby Union, was carried away by the buoyancy of the occasion.

At the post-match press conference, Berbizier was asked how his team could beat South Africa and New Zealand on their home soil and then crumble against England and Scotland. 'Perhaps we have had black jerseys on our minds because our vision has been black.' When asked if it was a disaster for French rugby, he replied, 'After the rain there is always sunshine. At the moment it is raining very heavily on the French team. Now we must find a patch of blue sky.' The French coach was looking decidedly soggy himself. A rainbow would now be urgently needed for the World Cup just three months away.

The streets of Paris were a sight to behold that night. At every turn there was a staggering Scotsman in a kilt. Delirious celebrations apparently took place back in the Scottish Borders and I have it on good authority that even Bill McLaren shared a wee dram with his beloved wife Bette.

'I'm a domesticated animal, Gawrrrdon,' he told me at training. 'I'll be on the first plane out of Paris after the game. I'm a homebody. I like to put my feet up in front of the fire.' And what a wonderfully warm feeling that must have been on the night of 18 February 1995 when Scotland finally exorcised a rugby demon.

What More Did They Have to Do?

The first Wallaby touring team ever to return home unbeaten. Twelve matches, twelve wins. Fifty-five tries to just fourteen against. Test wins over Italy, Scotland, Ireland and Wales followed by a spectacular final flourish against the Barbarians. So, was the 1996 European tour a triumphant campaign? No sir! Not according to the critics.

IN BRITAIN several rugby commentators suggested the 1996 Wallabies were only a shadow of the great Aussie sides of the previous twelve years. Their argument was that the tourists' game-plan was based on forward power to the point of obsession, while in the backs the great playmakers such as Farr-Jones and Lynagh had sadly passed on with no apparent replacements on the horizon.

Writing in the *Independent*, rugby correspondent Chris Hewett said: 'The Wallabies return home with a Triple Crown in their back pocket to go with the Grand Slam of '84. There the comparison ends. The Australians have far to travel to recreate the glory of the great days.' After the enjoyable spectacle between the NZ Barbarians and England at Twickenham played the day before Australia took on Wales, another London scribe suggested that either team would have had the measure of the Wallabies. How generous! The Kiwis were a scratch side—admittedly a brilliant one—but they hadn't played for five weeks. England, on the other hand, treated the game as a Test match and in the wash-up, almost self-destructed. Two weeks later the same Pommie team just managed to fall over the line 20–18 against a far-from-impressive Argentina.

But it wasn't only the UK press which got stuck into our squad. Touring Australian journalists Peter Jenkins and Greg Growden, both experienced and respected rugby writers, were critical of several key aspects of the Wallaby campaign. Among their concerns were the continual changing of personnel in the Test team, playing people out of position, and a failure to utilise the potent attacking options out wide.

Unfortunately, relations between coach Greg Smith and the two writers deteriorated during the second half of the tour. Smith was also having to cope with criticism coming from other directions. Bob Dwyer continually sniped at Smith's methods in both the Sydney press and his English newspaper column. As well, additional negative comment about the Wallaby management was attributed to Queensland coach John Connolly. This was allied to stories also appearing in the Australian press that there was a serious push from Queensland to bring down the whole Smith reign if the Wallaby coach dropped a Test match in Britain. (Towards the end of the tour the theme of that whispering campaign had changed to '. . . if they drop a *game*.') Yet another strong rumour suggested there was a move by senior players for a changing of the guard in favour of Rod Macqueen.

Rarely can a successful touring party have had to deal with such consistently negative media. It's difficult to imagine what more the team, coaching staff and management could have achieved. Yet despite their clean sweep, the carping, negative press in Australia did have the effect of undermining the immense overall achievement of John Eales' Wallabies. Smith found himself a coach under siege but, to his credit, he didn't adopt a 'siege mentality'. He pressed on without being distracted from his personal rugby convictions. There were plenty of doubters— some even within the team itself—but by tour's end, it was Smith and Eales who had the last laugh. So how was this success achieved?

The 1996 Wallabies in Britain played a far more physical game than any of their predecessors. The concept of smashing and overpowering the opposition forwards up the centre of the field in the first half of each contest was a punishing policy, but it worked. The men in gold finished over the top of all opponents, in many cases coming from behind. This fierce, confrontational approach demanded greater physical fitness, explosive power, and heightened mental strength. The high casualty rate in the pack on tour was clearly a by-product of this 'body-on-the-line' game-plan.

However, as the Wallabies demonstrated so ably in the second half of their clash with South Africa at Bloemfontein earlier in the year, such an approach needs swift modification against a side as physically strong up-front as the Springboks (or England for that matter). Hence the decision on that day to run the ball at every opportunity. There's little doubt the Australians would have won that match in the high veldt had it gone another five minutes.

With due respect to Bob Dwyer and his outstanding record as Australian coach, the 1996 Wallabies had a lot more steel and grit than the 1995 outfit which performed so limply at the World Cup in South Africa. The defensive effort of Smith's team on the European campaign was outstanding.

In hindsight it may have been the major foundation stone of the unbeaten tour. No opponent scored more than two tries in any one match. The Wallabies worked very hard on this aspect of their game-plan. On the rare occasions their line was breached it was refreshing to see how much the players actually 'hurt' and how readily they bounced back to regain the initiative. (It's also worth pointing out here that South Africa paid Australia's defence an enormous compliment in Bloemfontein by selecting a kicking scrum-half, Johan Roux, instead of Joost Van der Westhuizen, the best running No. 9 in the game. They had acknowledged that over the top of the Wallaby defence was a much easier route than through or around it. Roux's kicking in the first half played a crucial part in their narrow victory.)

By the end of the European campaign the team was as closely knit as any Wallaby side I can recall. There were no Qld/NSW cliques. John Eales and, possibly to a greater extent, Tim Horan and Brett Robinson, made sure of that.

In this regard champion centre Jason Little also made an interesting observation to me at the end of the tour. He pointed out that the ACT Brumbies' experience had been an infectious benefit for the whole tour party. Jason was referring to the Brumbies' set-up under Rod Macqueen in Canberra which brought Queenslanders and New South Welshmen together under one roof for more than two months. The Brumbies built a fantastic team spirit—the friendships and bonding established during the Super Twelve campaign set a shining example for everyone during the Wallabies' European campaign.

The introduction of a new national coaching staff in 1996 naturally brought new ideas, fresh enthusiasm and quite unprecedented competition for Test places. But with change comes risk, and it wasn't until the Australians' brilliant match against Munster (55–19) that Greg Smith's fortunes could genuinely be said to have passed the turning point. I have no doubt that the so-called second-string side that day would have been more than a handful for Scotland, Ireland or Wales. Writing in the *Irish Times*, esteemed rugby correspondent Edmund Van Esbeck didn't hold back:

> In the end, the crowd was left to admire and wonder at the awesome brilliance of the tourists as they scored nine tries, some beautifully created and splendidly executed. Forward power, superb teamwork, back-line flair, and pace and perception that will live long in the memories of those who witnessed it. The monument to achievement at Thomond Park yesterday was not built by Munster, it was erected by this superb performance from the Australians.

All Black coach John Hart was right on the money when he stated that Australian rugby was the major beneficiary of the inaugural Super Twelve season which preceded the European tour. Our rugby could justifiably claim that its international depth had reached new levels. Allowing for the injured back home the Wallabies could boast a genuine Test squad of more than thirty players for the first time in their history.

In truth, the Wallabies were in a rebuilding phase during 1996. Thirty-four players were given their chance at Test level. Not once in twelve Tests did Australia field the same side! Comfort zones for Test players were not in the Greg Smith doctrine. You performed or you were out. But if a player was dropped it was always made clear that it was just for that match. Only Matt Burke and David Wilson played every Test in 1996. Critics argued that a successful team needs to be a stable one, as demonstrated by our two great southern hemisphere rivals. The All Blacks prospered with their familiar starting line-up of stars, while the Springboks were able to string together five Test wins at the end of 1996 with the same combination.

Coach Smith and his fellow selectors opted for an alternative strategy right from the start. In their quest for a new-look team capable of rescaling the heights, they were prepared to experiment, often with players out of position. Some worked, some didn't. But none of those concerned could complain the moves had a negative effect on their outlook or selection chances. All should have become better players for the experience. In the most blatant case—the selection of Tim Horan on the wing—'The Sneak' would be the first to admit that it was time for him to reappraise his approach at inside centre. When given another chance, against Ulster, he took it. In essence Smith wanted Horan to attack the advantage line rather than pursuing a link role—a return to his halcyon days before the shattering knee injury in 1994 against Natal. By the end of the tour Horan was playing like the prince of old, causing havoc among the opposition with his aggression and searing pace.

Despite initial reservations, I became convinced that Smith's radical approach would ultimately prove to be a long-term success for the Wallabies. As tactical substitutions become more critical in rugby the team with a ready-made supply of versatile, high-impact replacements should prosper. Talent depth and strong levels of multi-skilling are the way of the future in the professional era. Ric Charlesworth proved it with our Olympic gold medal women's hockey team. He fielded not just eleven team members but sixteen great players, all interchangeable. Why not rugby? Selection stability will eventually evolve once the players tune into this new wavelength. Nevertheless, I doubt the Wallabies would have won all their games on the 1996 tour if such a large number of players hadn't been blooded during the year. They thrived in an atmosphere where they were always in contention for a Test spot.

In the course of rebuilding a team will endure setbacks. But credit where it's due. In Scotland the Australians were forced to maul (a tactic that went unchallenged) because the locals were so good at killing the ball. The Test against the Irish was dominated by the two forward packs. Aided by a strong wind in the first half the locals produced one of their special days at Lansdowne Road. Even when our scrum took the upper hand in the second half Australia made heavy weather of their victory. In fact, our backline didn't really come into its own until the Munster game. At Cardiff Arms Park against Wales the Australians were, in truth, a 25-to-30-point better side on the day. With the Wallabies leading 18–9 and poised to move to 25–9 in the fifty-third minute, Gareth Thomas's intercept try turned the match on its head. Yet so confident of their superiority were the men in gold that stand-in skipper Horan elected to ignore gift three-pointers in the cause of scoring tries.

It's worth remembering that Dwyer's much-vaunted Wallabies lost three matches in Britain in 1992, including their match against Munster. That these transitional 1996 Wallabies emerged without a stutter from their long European campaign was a monumental achievement. What more did they need to do?

Whether or not Smith's men would have beaten England to complete a Grand Slam is irrelevant. The Wallabies assessed each opponent on its merits and then pursued a winning strategy.

The back-up brains trust of Jake Howard, Alec Evans and Lloyd Walker did a mighty job and deserves high praise. In particular, the combined knowledge and expertise of Howard and Evans must be the envy of most of our opponents.

Highly skilled manager Peter Falk, through his sheer enthusiasm and sensitivity, was a star performer. But the reality is that the whole support team did a magnificent job. 'Doc' Best, physio Malcolm Brown, video analyst Scott Wisemantel, trainer Dirk Williams and gear steward John MacKay deserve the highest praise.

Greg Smith is not a self-promoter. He's an astute, honest, hard-working and extremely dedicated coach with a wickedly dry sense of humour. 1996 may have been a steep learning curve but it would be foolish to sell him short.

Sure, he made mistakes, but his squad won sixteen of their nineteen matches despite a horrendous start to the Tri-Nations series against the All Blacks in Wellington. Doesn't that suggest some very special qualities exist in this current crop of Wallabies and those steering their fortunes?

What's needed now on the road to 1999 is more of the same inspiration from the Munster example, a more concerted effort to implement the explosive attacking skills of Matt Burke, Joe Roff and co, less predictability and more of the element of surprise, and a hearty dose of mutual understanding between quiet achiever Smith and the demanding Australian media.

GORDON BRAY'S TOUR AWARDS

Outstanding Player: David Wilson

Best Comeback: A dead-heat—Tim 'Lazarus' Gavin as a second rower and David 'Nellie' Campese

Best Win: 55–19 victory over Munster

Most Brilliant Individual Performance: Matthew Burke v the Barbarians

Most Improved: Cameron Blades and Stephen Larkham

Most Disappointing Performance: All referees encountered except Ed Morrison

Merit Off-field Performance: Tim Horan serving snacks complete with stewardess apron to captain and officers on return flight to Australia

Quote of the Tour: 'I wonder what she does here during the week? Probably reads magazines.' Greg Smith during the visit to Buckingham Palace to meet the Queen.

Most Embarrassing Moment: John Eales doing his 'piece to camera' for Seven News at Edinburgh Castle. (By the fourteenth 'take' a large throng of fascinated tourists had surrounded the Australian skipper.)

Best Test Debut: David Giffin v Wales

Best Initiative: Physiotherapist Malcolm Brown, who took his physio table along to training sessions for outdoor treatment (only on sunny days). It was popular with several forwards who I suspect were really enhancing their tans to avoid another murderous session.

Best Initiative by an Opponent: Thirteen-man line-out employed by Connacht, which resulted in a last-minute try

Most Spectacular Try: Matthew Burke v Barbarians and Sam Payne v Munster

Most Inspired Gesture: Inviting H.G. Nelson to attend the final happy hour in London

Most Valuable Player: John Eales

The Snail Award: David Knox who slunk over for his first Test try (against Ireland), eleven years after making his debut against Fiji

Most Conscientious Award: Andrew 'The Ox' Heath. Before the Ulster game he chased referee Ken McCartney out of the dressing-room because the Scotsman hadn't checked his boots. (The Ox was later rebuked by Jake Howard who told him that any front rower worth his salt always had two pairs of boots. One to show the ref—and the other to play in.)

• •

Scores from the record books can sometimes hide the real story.

Australia may have lost all three games to New Zealand during the 1938 series, but the second Test at the Brisbane Exhibition Ground is still regarded as one of the finest-ever spectacles between the two countries.

Wallaby coach 'Johnnie' Wallace, who'd captained the 1927–28 Waratahs, described the match as the best he'd seen on Australian soil.

During that epic encounter Drummoyne fullback Ronald Rankin started a new fashion by wearing a strip of adhesive bandage across his nose. He was later selected for the 1939 Wallabies, who arrived in Britain only to have all their tour fixtures cancelled because of the outbreak of World War II.

But that wasn't the end of Rankin's bad luck.

He was finally chosen to lead the Wallabies to New Zealand in 1946, but broke his ankle at training on the eve of departure.

It would be enough to make a man take up croquet.

▪ ▪

Rugby
People

Stockbroker Andrew Stoddart had the honour of captaining his country in both cricket and rugby. The Blackheath and Harlequins back is also credited with being the first man to kick a goal from a mark in international rugby. Stoddart toured Australia with WW Read's 1887–88 cricketers and made 285 against Melbourne Juniors. He then packed away his cricket kit but stayed on in Australia to join Robert Seddon's touring British rugby side. Stoddart took over the captaincy after Seddon's fatal boating accident on the Hunter River.

Cliff Morgan—the Master

I could probably count them on one hand—the people who've made a lasting impression on me over three decades of broadcasting. The former great Welsh stand-off, Cliff Morgan, is near the top of that list.

AFTER a distinguished career in the fifties featuring an outstanding tour of South Africa in 1955, rugby maestro Cliff Morgan turned to broadcasting—and brought to the commentary box the same brilliance he had displayed on the field. The nuggety little Welshman's television description of the Barbarians versus the Seventh All Blacks match in 1973 at Cardiff Arms Park remains a broadcasting classic.

So many television commentators today describe the picture rather than complement it. Cliff was a Grand Master when it came to understated excitement behind the microphone. He could make a backline movement sparkle through intonation and subtle use of his voice. Morgan was also a professional from the old school of 'wordsmith' television commentators. He had the skills to adapt to a live telecast of a Royal wedding or State funeral if required.

After admiring his work for so long, I finally had the opportunity to meet him in person on the 1981–82 Wallaby tour of the UK and Ireland. At that time Cliff was Head of BBC Outside Broadcasts and I sought him out for a radio preview.

GB: *Cliff, what are you looking forward to most from this Wallaby tour?*

CM: Well, Gordon, the thing I look forward to most is the clash at the National Stadium between the Wallabies and Wales and, in particular, the confrontation of the two stand-offs. Our own William Gareth Davies—to me the Chapel of fly-halves. So much time, serenity and beautiful motion. And your own Mark Ella—a very busy player, instinctive, unpredictable—with the best still to come. If you like it's the Catholic versus the Unorthodox!

Alas, the tour selectors didn't see things the same way as Cliff, and his dream confrontation never eventuated. For his part, Davies captained Wales to victory over the Seventh Wallabies by 18–13. The Australian backs lacked imagination that day while the undermanned forward pack struggled for parity in the set pieces. (Ella was selected for the next International against Scotland—in my opinion, one Test too late.)

I've since met Cliff three times on Wallaby tours. Our next encounter was in 1984 just before the epic Grand Slam Test against England at Twickenham. I was rushing to the commentary box and his cheery words immediately stuck in my mind.

'Remember, Gordon, silence is golden!'

Seven years later I was again in the UK preparing for the television broadcast of the World Cup Final between Australia and England. The BBC had arranged a live hook-up between myself and Norman 'Nugget' May (who'd handed the rugby commentary to me in 1980). It was unexpected, and very emotional. Norman's last words to me were, 'Go for Gold, Gordo!' It was just the inspiration I needed, and the magnificent Wallabies didn't let us down.

I remember little of the commentary or the game. Somewhere in the back of my mind was the thought that this final would be the last major rugby telecast on the ABC. I didn't want to believe it and instead focused on Cliff's advice from 1984: 'Use the crowd and the atmosphere. Flow *with* it, don't fight it. And remember: breathing space!'

My last encounter with Cliff occurred the following year on the Wallaby tour of Ireland, Wales and England. I'd been recording a piece at the BBC in London and was in Portland Place waiting for a cab when a familiar voice quipped, 'You're not going to the Wallaby hotel by any chance are you, Boyo?' Minutes later Cliff and I were chugging along through peak-hour traffic in the back of a London cab. Always the opportunist, my tape recorder was rolling, and I've treasured the tape of that conversation ever since:

GB: *(Testing one, two, three . . .) We're just passing Oxford Circus on our way to the St Ermins Hotel. Alongside me in this taxi is the great Cliff Morgan. Cliff, what are your recollections of Cardiff 1973, Baa Baas v the All Blacks?*

CM: Vivid! The strange thing was of course that I wasn't the commentator, really. Bill McLaren was supposed to be doing the match. I'd been walking around Cardiff visiting a few pubs on the Friday when I received word that Bill had lost his voice. Suddenly I was asked, would I do this game? Of course I said yes. You know, when you've had a few beers you say yes to *anything*.

Next day turned out to be one of the most remarkable,

explosive, brilliant games I'd ever seen. I saw that day all the joys and tribulations of sport rolled into this wondrous occasion. There was style, there was hardness. The All Blacks played damn well in the second half and, funnily enough, could have won the game I believe if they'd played Sid Going at scrum-half.

It was a great match and I will never forget standing there and seeing that extraordinary move. [The amazing 90-metre Barbarian's try which most rugby enthusiasts believe is still the greatest try ever scored.]

It's still in my mind, you know. I can see the ball kicked ahead by Bryan Williams. I can see Phil Bennett gather and sidestep—*three* sidesteps—and then a pass. Suddenly there's a hooker involved. It went to J.P.R. Williams, who passed it on to John Pullin. I then see John Pullin slipping it down to Dawes. Did Dawes do a dummy? Yes he did. You don't do a dummy with your body being obvious. You use your eyes, and his eyes looked as if he was going to pass. *That* was the dummy!

Then inside to Tom David. Then Tom to Derek Quinnell. Then Derek threw it to John Bevan on the wing. But the ball was intercepted by a team-mate. Someone, for me, who is the greatest rugby player I've ever watched in my life, Gareth Edwards. And then he did what he was taught to do by his games master at school. He went and went, and then dived from six yards out. Because you've *got* to dive. If anybody tackles you, the try is still scored. That, for me, was absolutely wonderful. I will never forget it.

GB: *I thought your commentary of that try, which is still arguably the best try of all time, was a masterpiece . . . due mainly to the understated controlled excitement you conveyed. It was like releasing air from the neck of a party balloon before the final mad flourish.*

CM: Yes, it was understatement. The point is, that I went into the commentary box that day without a program, I had nothing. But I'd been living with the Lions on tour the year before and knew everybody. I wasn't a brilliant commentator, but I knew their backsides and the back of their heads. I didn't have to have a program or a number on the back. So I could then indulge myself in what I am so arrogantly good at doing—talking.

I was commentating on the game as if I was talking to someone in a pub over a glass of beer. I just did what I saw. I think also in television there are too many commentators who state the obvious: 'the ball is being passed and it goes to so and so.' You must build *expectation*. You say I called it well. I called it well because I knew the boys. That's one of the joys of being part of rugby. To know the players. I got to know so many smashing people in the world.

GB: *How do you rate this Australian team under Bob Dwyer, the current World Champions?*

CM: I'll tell you what this Australian team has got and what Australian rugby has given to the world in the last seven or eight years. It's given the little impulse to young kids. And I'm a great believer in young people learning by copying, you see. It's given them the impulse to be adventurous. To *dare*, not to do what the book says. I promise you that 80 per cent of international rugby is predictable. Forwards and backs all working to numbers. That is the most refreshing thing of all about you Australians.

Bob Dwyer has the ammunition. You have very good, big forwards. John Eales for me did the one tackle in the World Cup. I thought at the time, 'He's saved this game', because that, for me, was the worst game Australia played in the whole World Cup. They should have scored forty points that day and they didn't quite do it. The Wallabies have given the world that feeling of 'I'm going to be adventurous'. I don't believe in the predictability of numbers and passing. Let's do something that will shake them up. You've got a classic example with Campese. He *ventures*, and I love that.

Let me add just one thing. I mentioned Gareth Edwards as being the best player in the world. Australia has a man who I could name for his greatness. He hasn't just played scrum-half, but he's directed operations. He pointed into the loose rucks where the forwards should go. Where do I need this help? Nick Farr-Jones, for me, was the greatest player in the world for three seasons, and the saddest thing for me is that he is retiring. Yet at the same time I'm joyful because he's going out when he is still playing like a king.

So that's what Australian rugby has given me. I hope it doesn't lose that sense of adventure because that is the most important thing in the game. The ability to think spontaneously. The thing that lifts the spirits and makes you jump from your seat, that makes your mouth go dry. It's a moment to savour like David Campese's try against Wales last week. It came in the last second and—you know what?—he plucked the ball one-handed out of the air! The game needed it. Until then it had all been a bit humdrum in a sense. But then Campese lifted my spirits.

All too soon, our taxi pulled up at St Ermins Hotel. My spirits had also been lifted, by a man of vision with that special Welsh way with words—and a passion for his chosen sport.

Esala Teleni

When you consider that rugby is Fiji's national game, it's not hard to understand the deep sense of shock in this proud South Pacific island state when its team failed to qualify for the 1995 World Cup. Their coach at the time was Esala Teleni and he had to bear the full force of Fiji's disappointment.

SINCE its 1995 setback, former All Black prop Brad Johnstone has picked up the reins of Fijian rugby and his tough, no-nonsense coaching approach has produced some stunning results. In 1996 Fiji notched up a staggering 60–0 win over Western Samoa, but perhaps more impressive was a tenacious display at Loftus Versfeld in their first ever Test match against South Africa. The Springboks only really took control in the last fifteen minutes.

Johnstone has led Fijian rugby through the first tentative steps of professionalism by signing New Zealand-based Fijians to contracts with the national governing body. Easing away from the traditional focus on home-based talent, the ex-All Black has concentrated on wooing back the more 'developed' overseas players. Fiji can now confidently set about regaining their World Cup place in Wales for 1999. But it will still be a fine balancing act. Super League is cashed-up and eager to secure the cream of local talent. Fijian rugby is a national treasure and its great heritage must be preserved. Prime Minister Rabuka should ensure the game is not ravaged by the thirteen-a-side scouts.

In the mid-1980s, Esala Teleni captained Fiji from No. 8 between assignments as a patrol boat commander in the Fijian Navy. Not surprisingly, this excellent rugby player instilled discipline in his team and provided strong leadership. While in Australia in 1985, Teleni's Fijians gained respect for the courage and resourcefulness they displayed in their twin International losses. (This same team was unlucky not to beat Ireland at Lansdowne Road, and had a swag of victories over leading Welsh sides.)

Esala Teleni is now Commander of the Fiji Military and his record as a coach equates to one of military precision. His former club team, Fiji Army, at one point had not lost a local league match in five years—eighty straight victories! He is one of the truly inspirational figures of Fiji rugby. I spoke with him while he was still national coach during the ill-fated 1995 World Cup build-up aboard the Fiji army's team bus en route from hotel to stadium at the Malaysian Tens.

'My club mates have nicknamed me "Mr Mean" because they know when we talk business, it's *real* business,' he began. He proved to be a man with a gentle façade, but a strong disciplinarian, one who was more concerned with attitude than ability. 'I've kicked some very good players out of both the Army and Suva teams which I coach—probably about ten to fifteen. I'll warn players, but if they're late for training or the attitude is not there, they're out.' Teleni and his players enjoyed mutual respect and it was the sort of foundation that allowed him to overhaul Fiji's rugby fortunes in a very short time. Untouchable in the seven-a-side game, Fiji's fifteens performances had, however, been disintegrating. After humiliating losses in the 1992 Super Six series to Auckland (38–10) and New South Wales (52–6), they then suffered the indignity of losing to both Tonga and Western Samoa in the Triangular Series. The result of these lapses was that they missed a berth in the inaugural Super Ten tournament. The coach and manager resigned.

Call it a military coup if you like, but Major Esala Teleni was then invited to be interim coach for the upcoming matches against the junior Springboks and the Maoris. 'Fijian rugby was too preoccupied with sevens. That was a major factor in our demise,' said Teleni. 'At the start of last season our country was still celebrating another Fijian triumph in the Hong Kong Sevens. It was not an ideal platform for the Super Six. When I was invited to take over, I asked for a full review of the selectors. A totally new panel was then brought in. We retained only five players, and youngsters with a hungry attitude were given their chance.'

Fiji has always had an abundance of naturally-talented players with exceptional ball skills. Teleni's focus was on picking the best players available and ensuring they played in their right positions. 'I was lucky that my new squad had good match fitness. From the start I told our players we were resorting to our natural game of opening out in the backs and providing plenty of support. We knew that the Junior Springboks wouldn't like us running at them so our strategy was to do just that.'

A thirty-point victory over the young South Africans served notice that Fijian rugby was back on course. 'We used plenty of mini-rucks and mini-mauls. I stood the flankers out on the backs to make midfield gains and create overlaps wider out. By not committing all our forwards we were able to use tight forwards as backs as well.' There was also significant improvement in set pieces, particularly the scrum. After seeing their forward pack pushed about and harassed earlier in the season, the Fijian public was delighted to see a new resolve 'up-front'.

'To maintain a running game we had to hold our scrum,' Teleni said. 'In the last World Cup we managed to hold our scrum but it didn't last. There were problems with fitness. Programs were introduced but they weren't carried through properly. The players were thinking they were fit but they really weren't. We've introduced a weights program over the past few years to build the strength and power of our forwards. It paid off against the Springboks.'

The clash with the Maoris in November 1992 was a heartbreaker for the Fijians. A last-ditch conversion was missed by fly-half Ella Rokowalloa, resulting in a one-point win for the Kiwis. 'We used the same approach against the Kiwis and played very well too,' Teleni said. 'The 16,000 fans in Suva left the ground happy after witnessing a thrilling spectacle.'

Esala's devotion to 'the real business' of coaching grew naturally from his years of duty in Fiji's Senior Service. 'When I was in the navy we would visit our islands and I'd take the chance to coach schoolkids and the local men, whenever possible. That's where my love of coaching grew. Today, the army is very accommodating when I am required for coaching duties. I'm now working with all the provincial coaches and the leading club coaches to focus on our traditional style of rugby. We are sending promising players from outlying areas to strong clubs. When the players arrive for national squad sessions they're all focused on our running pattern of play, whereas previously I was trying to mix a host of different coaching approaches. The response has been very positive and I'm receiving terrific support.'

Teleni was seen by most in Fiji as the rugby Messiah—the man to lead his nation out of the wilderness. Unlike many Fijian rugby officials, he pays tribute to George Simpkin who assisted in their 1991 World Cup campaign. 'George tried to show us how to win possession. However, most of the coaches took it the wrong way, concentrating solely on his ideas and forgetting to use our natural Fijian skills. But George did a marvellous job.'

As to the experimental ruck/maul law, he hoped it would stay. 'We've struggled to hold the rolling mauls of countries like New Zealand and Australia. We want to keep the ball alive and moving. That's our game.'

Indeed it is—and it's a fresh, free-wheeling style of rugby the rest of the world enjoys and admires.

Postscript

In 1993 Fiji were defeated 21–10 by the touring Scotland team. A subsequent 24–11 loss to Tonga meant they had to win the return match by more than 13 points to qualify for the 1995 World Cup.

Fiji won 15–10 and were thus eliminated, with Tonga joining neighbouring Western Samoa in South Africa. Teleni departed for naval college in England to further his career.

In 1994 Nadroga coach Mele Kurisaru took over the national position with Brad Johnstone as his technical adviser.

Esala Teleni has returned to Fiji after his two-year secondment in England and has become Commander of the Fiji military forces. He is again coaching successfully in Suva.

The recent encounters between rugby league and rugby union in the UK, together with the reinvigorated competition for crowds between the two codes in Australia, have again raised the old issue of tribal loyalties and class distinctions.

It's instructive to remember the views of 1908 Wallaby captain, Dr Herb 'Paddy' Moran. He witnessed the trauma of the league breakaway first hand and always believed that it was the new professionals who had created the social divisions in Australian football.

In his classic memoirs *Viewless Winds* Moran explained that at the turn of the century rugby was a game for all classes—there were no social distinctions.

'We tussled with factory hands and firemen, with miners, wharf labourers and carters,' he wrote of his early playing days with Sydney University.

'These players might have rougher manners but in many of the elementary virtues of life they were our superiors. When professionalism came, we were shut out from friendships with men in ranks called 'lower' and our education suffered.

'We were sentenced to be weaker in humanity.'

The humble Corinthian ethic of those sentiments from almost a century ago is food for thought again today.

John Maxwell

There is always a special magic about Coogee Oval with a big crowd in. Maybe it's because the Randwick ground is flanked by flats and home units on three sides. When the Galloping Greens took on the All Blacks back in 1988 every vantage point was taken, with about 9000 spectators inside and at least another 2000 outside on rooftops, balconies and hanging out of windows. Gallant Randwick were ultimately outscored three tries to one but not before they'd given the Kiwis a typical no-holds-barred welcome to Coogee.

IT WAS a sight that brought tears to the eyes of club veteran John Maxwell. 'Maxy' is a truly passionate rugby man. When it comes to his beloved 'Myrtle Green' it would be difficult to meet a more dedicated clubman. Randwick rugby has been Maxwell's ongoing love affair for more than three decades; first as a young fan, next as a stalwart player and now as its highly respected first-grade coach. In his twenty-one years as a player John figured in fourteen first-grade grand finals for an amazing ten wins. Although he captained Australia to victory at the Hong Kong Sevens, the Randwick iron man never achieved senior national honours. Sadly, he had to decline an invitation from Bob Dwyer to tour with the Wallabies to New Zealand in 1982 because his fledgling printing business had to take priority.

In his fourth season as first-grade coach in 1996, John Maxwell brought Randwick from fifth spot in the finals series to premiership honours—his second such success. That feat of typical, single-minded application took me back to an article I'd written after a conversation we'd had before his debut year as the Greens' senior coach.

After 428 grade games for the 'Galloping Greens' since 1972, John Maxwell is officially hanging up his boots, 'for this year anyway'. In a surprise move, Maxwell displaces Jeff Sayle as first-grade coach of Australia's most famous and successful club team. He'll also handle the role of club coach.

But why the change? After all, Randwick has won the last six first-grade premierships, the last five under Sayle. 'Traditionally, Randwick has played a running game. We've moved the ball wide and achieved success with classic tries, often by our wingers,' John Maxwell says. 'In recent years though the club has drifted away from the adventurous approach to a tighter pattern relying on forward dominance. Because it's been successful, you go with the strength. However, I believe there's been a cost. The club is in danger of losing its heritage.'

From his junior days when he used to watch greats like Ken Catchpole 'down at Coogee', the Randwick ideology has been ingrained in Maxwell.

'As a youngster I was greatly impressed by these old guys who'd impart their vast knowledge. Former players, people like Cyril Towers, who'd initiated and founded the concept of running rugby. I realised it was something special to belong to. Each step along the way was tremendously exciting. Coming into grade, then winning premiership after premiership and deriving so much enjoyment, and representative selection. I can honestly say, though, this latest coaching appointment has given me my biggest thrill.'

There will inevitably be a degree of resistance at Randwick. Why change something that's been working successfully? Maxwell has the perfect reply: 'I believe in this change of direction for the players' sake because they will get more enjoyment. We want a continuity-based game. Randwick's running brand of rugby originally exposed the club to great success. My philosophy is, even if we aren't successful, we're trying to play a brand of rugby *everyone* would like to play. If that brings us success in winning competitions, so be it. If it doesn't we're still successful because we're trying to continue the proud history of the club.'

So where does the change of direction leave Jeff Sayle and Alan Gaffney? According to Maxwell, they'll both play vital roles within the club as coaching coordinators. 'There's no way I'll ever be critical of the club because they've been guided by success—it's pushed them along a path. I believe in splitting the backs and forwards at training, which means Alan and Jeff will be responsible for all the teams because the club will be playing one style of football—running rugby. Personally, I didn't think the club was getting enough value out of Jeff Sayle just being first grade coach. I feel the club as a whole is going to get more rewards from this person with the knowledge he has, his charisma and the character he is. All the players will benefit—not just the top fifteen. I honestly believe that is Jeff's biggest asset to the club—his personality, just being himself, and his terrific knowledge. I'd like to think that the young people who are playing fourth grade are now going to have those benefits. It's not that he didn't want to give it in the past, he just didn't have the time. Jeff will still have an input into first grade. With this reorganisation, I feel I can be of more value to the club this year than I was last year as a player.'

Maxwell's credentials for the first-grade coaching job are impressive. He's played alongside some of Australia's greatest players. His career covers a significant portion of Randwick's proud seventy-year history. He's certainly in good company when you reflect on some of the club's favourite sons: Cyril Towers (1925–42), Nick Shehadie (1941–58) and Ken Catchpole (1959–71). He also enjoyed success at seven-a-side rugby as captain/coach of Australia's winning Hong Kong teams in 1982–83, which shows his versatility and adaptability—a necessary quality under the new laws.

'I think the new laws are perfect for the type of game we want to play. They don't provide security when you hang onto the ball in tight play. All the more reason to play a wider attacking game for eighty minutes. That doesn't mean you throw the ball around willy-nilly and play three-man rucks and mauls. It's all about control and developing a style of play which will allow you, for example, to secure the ball at the back of a maul where the referee can see it and won't "blow it up".'

'We'll certainly be kicking less. Put it this way: would you rather have Tim Kellaher kicking to you or running at you? Ball retention will be a priority. The new laws demand a smarter, more creative and more intelligent type of forward. You can't afford to lose concentration now and just plod along. You have to be more alert. That's the type of player we need to develop, one who is more aware how the game should be played, when to slow it up or when to speed it up.'

By his own definition, John Maxwell will be successful in 1993. He'll also succeed for other reasons. The final word on this ultimate clubman comes from Australian coach Bob Dwyer: 'He'd be down at Coogee putting up the hessian at 8.30 on a Saturday morning. He'd then run the line in fifth grade, go home and take his kids off to sport, and then he'd be back to play first grade. That's how much the Club means to him.'

John Maxwell has been as good as his word. In his first four seasons as first-grade coach, Randwick scored 460 tries: 99 in 1993, 128 in 1994, 115 in 1995 and 118 in 1996.

• •

There comes a time when even club loyalty has to go out the window.

In 1996 Gordon's sixth grade were a prop short for their game against Manly. So, in a truly sporting gesture, Manly's player-coach Russell 'Rusty' Mackie swapped his beloved red-and-blue jumper for the Gordon strip and packed down with the Highlanders.

To make matters worse, Russell then proceeded to score a try against his own team and help Gordon to a 23–0 lead.

Now that really was a bit rich, especially when Mackie had played twenty-six straight seasons and around 700 club games for the Seasiders.

But the story has a happy ending. Manly stormed home to snatch a dramatic 24–23 win, and the club management has had the good grace to reaffirm Rusty's shaky tenure on the sixth-grade coaching position.

Rugby is special.

• •

The late Dr Danie Craven, patriarch of South African rugby, was the grandson of a Yorkshire-born diamond prospector. 'The Doc' played sixteen Tests as a Springbok, and went on to become a legend as both a coach and administrator.

Seven of his Tests were against Australia, including four consecutive games in different positions. The remarkable sequence of jersey-changes ran as follows:

- In 1933, at Port Elizabeth, he played centre against the Wallabies (won 11–0).
- In the following Test, at Bloemfontein (lost 15–4), he returned to his customary spot at scrum-half.
- Four years later the Springboks were 'Down Under' and Craven played fly-half in the first Test at the SCG, won 9–5 by the tourists.
- Finally, in a surprise tactical move, he was then picked at No. 8 for the second International, won 26–17 by the South Africans.

The visitors' only loss on that eleven-match tour back in 1937 was to NSW in extremely muddy conditions.

Spearheaded by their brilliant centre, Cyril Towers, the Waratahs upset the tourists by adopting a spirited running game, despite the glue-pot paddock.

On a day they long remembered, the Springboks were not only out-foxed by the NSW backs, but given a thorough going-over at the hands of the Blues' famous pair of firebrand forwards, Aub Hodgson and 'Wild Bill' Cerutti.

Doc Craven

As the dominant figure in South African rugby this century Dr Danie Craven was internationally acknowledged as 'Mr Rugby'. Back in 1992 I led a supporter's tour group on the Wallabies' trek to South Africa. With his health failing fast, I seized what was probably my last chance to meet the 'Good Doctor'.

OUR VISIT to Stellenbosch University, Danie Craven's working home, was very special. Not only did it produce a private hearing with The Doc but he also joined our group for a heart-warming cocktail party in the rugby club. Proudly he showed off the grand collection of rugby memorabilia. His Springbok blazer, jumper and cap were showpiece items in what was a veritable history of the great university's rugby pedigree.

As player, coach and administrator Dr Craven's career is unparalleled in rugby history. He was at the helm of South African rugby through the hateful apartheid era. He was often outspoken, but first and foremost he remained a champion of his country's national game. His greatest joy was to see South Africa officially readmitted to rugby's international family after apartheid finally ended in 1992.

Our discussion, possibly his last recorded interview, took place in his study at Stellenbosch University.

GB: *What are your feelings now after the twin tours by Australia and New Zealand?*

DC: I am very grateful that the All Blacks and the Wallabies came to our country. They've not only left their mark on our game but our whole political situation. I don't think South Africa has been more united than they are after these two tours. From my viewpoint all the ills and hurts of the past have been removed because, politically speaking, we haven't been so well treated by Australia and New Zealand in the past. But the crowds have now let off steam—they've seen that your rugby players are like ours and links with Australia and NZ are now much closer. Particularly the Wallabies—they are fine men. I don't think we've ever had a better-behaved team. They're friendly, always helpful and always speaking to people. Nothing is too great a sacrifice for them.

The Wallabies still have adventure in their game—it's not just kicking and playing with the forwards. It's a fifteen-man game. We admire your flair. With a man like Campese it's a game of wit and the game of a fencer. Let the ball do the work and then you won't know where the attack will come from. But when you know it's only around the scrum or the fly-half then it becomes monotonous.

GB: *What are your feelings about the recent law changes?*

DC: This game should always be an adventure. Your man Dr Vanderfield changed the laws and made a very good job of it. In the All Blacks match there were only a handful of scrums in one half. That's the way it should be. Nobody

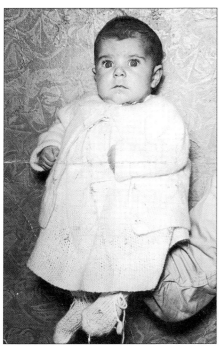

Left: Gordon Bray, the budding commentator. Eyes were on the ball at an early age.

Below: Sprung by the Sydney *Sun* newspaper. Alan Davidson's last Test in 1963 at the Sydney Cricket Ground. The author, playing truant in school uniform, clutches Wally Grout's wicket-keeping pad.
Photo: Fairfax Photo Library

Homebush Boys High School's only winning Waratah Shield team (1965). Middle row, third from the left is John Symond (MD Aussie Home Loans). Front row, second from the left is former Wests First Grader Greg Bell. That's the author second from the right, front row, alongside the legendary Jack 'Pug' Mason. *Photo: John Symond*

The 1976 Wallabies in action: *Sur le sol français*. 'Le Gunfighter' Steve Finnane and his fellow forwards secure a smooth release for scrum-half Rod Hauser against a French selection.

Steve 'Butcher' Finnane. Nicknamed 'Le Gunfighter' on the 1976 French tour. His walrus moustache, red beret, copy of *Playboy* and red apple are an enduring memory.

1976 French tour: the medieval castle in Perigeux and the treacherous pier — scene for a daring early morning escape by the author and Wallaby manager John Bain.

A fitting swansong for the ageless Michael 'Bread' Rowles after Easts' 1981 Third Grade grand final victory over Eastwood...'They wouldn't be able to lift me now!' *Photo: Michael Rowles*

Mark Ella on the warpath in his 1980 Test debut against the All Blacks at the Sydney Cricket Ground. *Photo: Action Photographics*

The Australian Schoolboy class of 1977-78. The magnificent combination of Mark Ella and Michael Hawker against the 1983 All Blacks. *Photo: Action Photographics*

Wallaby Manager's meeting in Cardiff, 1981. Left to right: David Lord, Frank O'Callaghan, Sir Nicholas Shehadie, Sinclair Robieson, Ian Telford and Gordon Bray.

Above: The calm before the Wallaby storm. Cardiff Arms park, 1984. Australia beat Wales 28-9 and scored their famous 'pushover' try. *Photo: Adrian Short*

Left: After the final whistle. Wallaby coach Alan Jones and future Seven commentator Simon Poidevin contemplate the 25-24 loss to the All Blacks at the SCG in 1984. *Photo: Action Photographics*

Above: Thomond Park Limerick, 1984: Munster vs Australia. At times visibility was down to ten metres.

Left: Munster match programme from the 1984 Grand Slam Wallaby tour. Coach Alan Jones master-minded a 'seeing-eye' strategy in the pea-soup fog.

On tour with the Classic Wallabies, Bermuda, 1990 – an unexpected international debut for the author! (Standing far right).
Photo: Peter Carson

Dressed to kill in Bermuda with the great 'Sir', Stanislaus Pilecki. 18 Tests and 128 games for Queensland – a rugby legend.
Photo: Peter Carson

A thorn between two roses — the Channel Seven commentary team. With Bledisloe Cup gladiators Chris 'Buddha' Handy, and Simon 'Mr Atlas' Poidevin.
Photo: Matt Brooks

likes watching a scrum which is a test of strength. It's now what it should be—a place where you can gain possession. We still have to alter the lineout and Roger will be wise enough to do that. I would suggest that in the quick lineout the ball can be thrown in anywhere providing it doesn't go forward. [Currently it must be thrown in straight]. It is important the team that didn't kill the ball can get an advantage. By and large, the game is now faster—it's a game of wit and outlasting your opponents by fair means. The Wallabies beat Northern Transvaal, who played well above themselves, by throwing the ball around when under pressure and they thoroughly deserved their victory.

GB: *What effect have these tours had on your vision for South African rugby?*

DC: We didn't know our strengths or our weaknesses. We've been barred from playing against other countries so we didn't know our capabilities. The important thing is we're back in world rugby and, by playing against stronger teams, we are raising the ceiling of our rugby. After our tours of France and England later this year we'll be ready for the 'big stuff' in Australia next year.

GB: *Are we soon going to see the the day when black Springboks will be a common sight?*

DC: Oh yes. They have much leeway to make up but I think the Coloureds are just about ready to come through. They have some fine players and there will be a few in the touring team to France. They'll emerge step by step. They too must learn a lot and gain the experience we've had over all the years—but we are working with them, they are playing with us. Since 1977 when we unified, they've been with us and the spirit of the game has spread over into their lives as it has ours—they're just like us. That is our next problem, to accommodate them one hundred per cent.

GB: *How do you explain your lifelong passion for the game?*

DC: It's a contact game—you can kill the man. But now they've got the touch judge watching. Still, you can do bad things to your opponent but you don't. I have a saying here, 'that you play as you live'. If I watch a player when he comes to Stellenbosch, after a practice or two, I can tell you what kind of man he is. Rugby has a stamp, a spirit: it's alive, and that spirit of rugby is one that should dominate everything—not winning, because that has become too important.

That is why we were opposed to the World Cup originally. We said it would encourage patriotism or nationalism at the expense of sportsmanship. If we're not careful that is what could happen to the game. Good players are so scarce that they have more or less turned professional without being called professionals. The game is heading that way. I'm sorry about that but it's something we can't stop. The trouble is that we are too weak. There is too much 'I' and 'me'. We have a team game and it is 'us' and 'we'. That is where we score over all individual sports. We are a team and we must continue to emphasise team spirit.

In 1992, Doctor Craven made a stirring farewell speech to the Wallabies at the post-Test match function at Newlands. He also chose a few words for his own Union:

'After this tour I will have a lot to say to our own people who didn't want to have a tour overseas, who shot me down in all places. It's no use when things go wrong to suppress. You've got to guide. South African rugby must be guided now—we've had enough suppression in our time.

'When we look at today's game, the Wallabies took every possible opportunity, and that is experience. I've never in all my life thanked a New Zealand referee, but to Mr Bishop [may I say] you did very well and thank you for the example you put to our referees on how to handle this game of rugby.

'What a change it's been with these tours. Not to see Northern Transvaal playing Western Province, Transvaal playing Natal and all that type of rubbish! We have now risen to a higher level, and that is the level I like and we all like.'

• •

The 1937 Springboks are still regarded as one of the greatest teams to leave South African shores. They won both their Test series against Australia and New Zealand, and lost just two of their twenty-six matches.

During the Australian leg of their tour the Springboks led a rather pampered life. They travelled on their own dedicated private train, complete with first-class dining facilities.

This luxurious mode of conveyance must have been quite an experience for the Springbok captain, Philip Nel.

Back home, when playing for his Collegians club in Natal, the big farmer had to first travel fifty kilometres by horseback, and then a further 125 kilometres by taxi just to reach Pietermaritzburg for his game. He undertook that journey every weekend.

■ ■

'Thrill 'em, but don't kill 'em'—that's the curious motto of former Wallaby forward coach John 'Jake' Howard. And no, it's not the distillation of some innovative personal rugby philosophy. The source of the motto is much more mundane. When he's not preoccupied with rugby matters, Jake Howard devotes his time to the family amusement ride business—those Ghost Trains and Whizzers that have thrilled generations of kids from backblock carnivals to the Royal Easter Show.

Howard's late father Bill jumped the rattlers during the Great Depression until he found work running the rides at country shows and before long he owned those rides. Jake hadn't even heard of rugby until his Dad packed him off to St Joseph's College in Sydney 'where I discovered it was the main religion'. Jake was good enough to make the great University side under legendary coach Dave Brockoff. At one point in the early 1970s the students had an incredible six of their First Grade Pack in the test side, including Howard at prop forward.

He remembers Brockhoff's unique approach to motivational coaching. They were playing a club game at Coogee Oval against Randwick. Unbeknownst to the players, Brock had carefully unscrewed the hinges of the dressing-room door. 'At the climatic moment, he wound up his emotional Anzac Day address with the words "Follow me boys!" before kicking the door down with a flourish. We won of course.'

Rugby had always been a way of life in the Howard household. His son Pat has already played 13 tests for the Wallabies and is currently starring for the ACT Brumbies. Wife Margarete is the daughter of the great Cyril Towers and a successful coach in her own right, inheriting her father's stern 'run-straight-at-em' approach to backline play.

By 1991 Jake was an assistant coach to Bob Dwyer for Australia's triumphant World Cup campaign. He stood down in 1993, but 'Howard's Way' lured him back to his beloved Wallabies in 1996.

In contrast to his colourful mentor from university days, the rugby Gospel According to Howard is delivered with understatement. 'The game may be more technical these days, but it hasn't changed all that much. Your job as coach is to get the simple messages across.

Thrill 'em and kill 'em Jake.

The Tribulations of Tiny Tim

1) Which well-known Wallaby forward stayed with the Queen's household at Windsor Castle during the 1991 World Cup?

2) Which Australian produced a key to the Castle from his trouser pocket on national TV just before the final at Twickenham?

The answer to both questions is, of course, Tim Gavin, a country bred rugby man with a special gift for overcoming unexpected adversity.

BACK IN 1991, Tim Gavin, the rangy Wallaby No. 8, had the wretched luck to be injured just before the Cup campaign. His elevation to royal lodgings was courtesy of his sister Jill, who just happened to be a groom for Prince Charles' polo ponies. The sadly sidelined Tim was a welcome 'expert' addition to our ABC-TV commentary team, although we certainly couldn't afford to pay for the standard of accommodation he seemed to expect.

'Gav' missed the original Wallaby selection for the Europe campaign in 1996, but was soon called over as a replacement. Once again he managed to enjoy the 'royal' treatment. But it's a long story . . .

I was outward bound from Sydney on QF1 with the Seven Network rugby team flying to London to join up with the touring Wallabies. The flight services director out of Bangkok introduced himself to me as a very keen supporter of Australian rugby. He very kindly suggested that if I wanted to stretch out, there was some room up in the 'sharp end' and he'd shift me there after the dinner service. The prospect of a decent sleep on long international flights is always inviting, so he didn't have to ask twice.

When the time came I was out of the blocks and slipping away from my sleepy colleagues the moment the cabin lights dimmed. After settling me into the very comfortable new surroundings the senior steward in first class informed me we'd met at Strasbourg in 1989 when the Wallabies had scored their famous win over France. But his next rather formal remark surprised me even more. 'Oh, and by the way Mr Bray, Tim Gavin is on the flight and he'll be joining you in a few moments. I do believe he played that day in Strasbourg.'

Gav duly arrived and any plans for sleep went straight out the window (or should I say porthole). After enjoying several 'night-caps' Tim decided he was a bit peckish. So, entirely against my better judgment, we tucked into a four-course silver service meal at what for us was 3.30 in the morning. The Iranian caviar was particularly appetising, but I'm still not so sure that those couple of cognacs afterwards to flush our digestive tracts were such an inspired notion. When we finally touched the tarmac at Heathrow Messrs Gavin and Bray were feeling a teensy bit tarnished, but suitably impressed with the quality of Qantas in-flight service.

We bid a temporary farewell because Tim was on an earlier shuttle flight to Edinburgh. My parting words were, 'Aren't you lucky you don't have to play tonight in Perth against the Scottish selection?' About an hour later I picked up a copy of the London *Daily Telegraph* in the departure lounge only to come across a rugby article titled, 'Replacement Gavin Straight into Wallaby Team.'

To make matters worse for our rugby hero, when the Seven crew arrived at Edinburgh, there was Tim Gavin still at the baggage carousel, now looking positively bothered, bewildered and harassed. He was still waiting for his luggage from the earlier flight. Gav eventually reached the Wallaby hotel—miles out of Perth, well after lunch. He duly played against the Scottish selection that night in David Giffin's boots, plus borrowed socks and shorts.

I'd managed to catch up with Tim just before the team bus set off for the game. His parting quip, 'This is my punishment,' was offered with a good-natured chuckle. But despite his recent gastronomic indulgences, lack of sleep over the previous forty-eight hours and misplaced baggage, Tim produced a vintage 'Keith Miller'-type performance. In atrocious conditions—freezing temperatures and driving rain—he won crucial lineout ball, pulled off big tackles and effected some secure hit-ups just when things were looking pretty shaky. In short, our brand new arrival was one of the best on the paddock.

Which goes to show: you can't hold a good man down, especially one from solid farming stock who's prepared himself carefully on a pre-match diet of fine Iranian caviar and the very best French cognac.

You'll need to have a pretty good long-term rugby memory to recall what David Campese and dynamic Easts open-side flanker Dirk Williams have in common.

They both played their first big game at the SCG in 1982—the trans-Tasman Under 21 curtain-raiser for the second Test between the Wallabies and Scotland.

No fewer than sixteen future Internationals came out of that match. Campo's team-mates in the Australian side included Michael Lynagh, Steve Tuynman and Tommy Lawton. Among Dirk's colleagues facing the young Aussies across the sacred old SCG turf were budding All Black greats Grant Fox and Steve McDowell.

The Australian Colts downed their New Zealand counterparts 36–12 and the teenage Campese so dazzled the selectors that his inclusion in the Wallaby team headed for NZ later that month was a mere formality. The rest is the stuff of rugby folklore.

From that day at the SCG fifteen years ago the fortunes of the two rugby stalwarts took contrasting courses, but they came together again in the 1996 Wallabies' unbeaten tour of Europe. Campo played two tests, while Williams served as fitness coach and even got a game in the green and gold when the side was decimated by injuries. He scored Australia's first try against a Scottish selection in Perth.

Michael Lynagh

I first saw Michael Lynagh play in 1980 as fly-half for the Australian Under 17 team against their Kiwi counterparts. Even at that formative stage of development he was a standout. He could already draw on a high skill level, on-field maturity well beyond his years and that priceless quality of appearing to have so much time in everything he did.

KNOWN AS 'Noddy'—though there was nothing sleepy about him on the field—Michael Lynagh went on to become one of our truly great players, but from the time he first wore the senior Queensland jumper in 1982 to his last Test campaign (as skipper of the 1995 World Cup squad), he remained a humble and studious young champion. In a masterly stroke of judgment, Alan Jones selected him at inside centre on the 1984 Grand Slam tour—an enormous call because it meant the exclusion of classy Michael Hawker. Although Lynagh's apprenticeship outside Mark Ella lasted just three months, it's hard to imagine a better transition to the coveted No. 10 Wallaby jumper.

Michael's leadership qualities reached their peak during the

1991 World Cup quarter-final against Ireland at Lansdowne Road. With captain Nick Farr-Jones sidelined through injury, Noddy's calmness in the midst of that maelstrom almost single-handedly steered the ailing Wallabies to their epic victory. His match-winning try in the dying stages is still perhaps the most important single score in Australian history.

A naturally brilliant ball player and runner, his silken skills were all too often kept under wraps in the Queensland jumper. How differently he might have developed as a youngster at Randwick! Nonetheless, if you had to judge contenders for the most complete fly-half ever, Michael Lynagh would be on any short list. And, as we discover in this 1993 interview, the shy young rugby player of the eighties had become very much his own man a decade later.

> **GB:** *Injury kept you out of the Bledisloe Cup match in Dunedin—the first time you've missed an All Black Test since 1988. Do you agree with the popular notion that the Wallaby build-up was inferior to New Zealand's?*

> **ML:** I think Australia was underdone, but having said that we always knew the Tongan Test was our only lead-up game and thus prepared to the best of our ability. After the heavy workload with the Super Ten series and the interstate games you could argue therefore that Australia would have been nice and fresh after just one Test. Having the benefit of hindsight we probably needed one more game, not necessarily a hard one but one together, just to fine-tune combination and skill levels, as a team.

> Watching the game, it took Australia a full twenty minutes to settle into the match. After that we became pretty competitive. I would have to say though that some of our guys looked just a little flat ... whether that's a symptom of too

much football in recent months or niggling injuries, I don't really know.

GB: *Is there a danger for Australia as world champions of falling into the same trap that beset NZ rugby after their 1987 World Cup triumph, that is, too much focus on off-field activities and financial considerations?*

ML: Well, we had a good year last year after winning the Cup in 1991. There was a lot of off-field activity going on yet we were still able to perform on the field. It's something we're aware of and we speak about. Everything comes back to performing on the field. If we feel that off-field activities are having an effect then we'll cut back.

GB: *The national governing rugby union bodies around the world are addressing the question of compensation for amateurs who are expected to perform as 'professional entertainers'. There has been talk of contracting players to the national unions. What's your reaction?*

ML: I know the ARU would love to be able to compensate the players more adequately and positive steps have been taken in that direction. I believe the national players should be paid a percentage of the gate, but I realise that money has already been earmarked for things such as development at junior level. The players are now getting a percentage of sponsorship, which is great. But, when you divide it up among a group of nearly forty, including officials, it's not a significant amount. It's a progressive step but more has to be done. The players are happy to give their time in return to sponsors, within reason, but this area still has to be fine-tuned.

Regarding the question of contracts, the Australian Rugby Union has placed bans on where a player can go and what he can do. I don't believe any union can 'own' a player without giving something back in the way of compensation.

I'm definitely in favour of a contractual set-up much the same as the cricket approach here in Australia, where national team members are contracted to the governing body on financial retainers. The problem for rugby union is, where does that money come from? I think a decision has to be made by the national rugby unions that if they want to control the players to the extent they do, then they have to go out and find the money.

GB: *You've now had two successful seasons with Benetton Treviso in Italy. Is 'spaghetti rugby' good for the code?*

ML: From a strictly playing viewpoint you'd have reservations. Especially when you look at the standard of some of the teams at the bottom of the first division and in second division. Discipline is a problem and so is the standard of refereeing. But certainly Benetton Treviso and Milan would hold their own in club football in Australia.

I can understand the argument of national unions who say Italian rugby is counter-productive to their own cause. However from my situation, I went over there two years ago after playing high-level rugby for about ten years and I was really starting to get stale . . . running around the same ovals, playing against the same teams, playing under the same coaches and so forth. Italy provided a new stimulus—a different culture, a new style of football and new people. When I came back last year I felt anything but tired. My enthusiasm had returned. I was really looking forward to being back alongside guys I'd missed playing with. The same thing applied this year. I came back feeling pretty fit and enthusiastic. I see it as a way of prolonging my involvement in the game. Your body and mind need a different environment and challenge when you've been at the same routine for a long time.

GB: *Newspaper reports indicate you haven't had too much sympathy from the Queensland Rugby Union. Has that been the case?*

ML: I haven't had the support, true, and I guess that's understandable, but I don't fully appreciate why. I've played ninety-five games for Queensland and have given loyal service. But as soon as you step out of line, away from the inner circle, you're ostracised. I can understand their point of view but I also feel I'm entitled to make my own decisions on my lifestyle and rugby career.

GB: *Do you think that rugby in Australia, particularly at interstate level, is too insular?*

ML: Definitely. Having stepped outside I've been able to look in more objectively. As a player I've often thought that Australian rugby suffers constantly at interstate level from the in-fighting, bickering and often bitter exchanges, at administration level, between Queensland and NSW. It seems to me that state interests are put before the national cause, which is obviously counter-productive. It's good to have a healthy rivalry but not when it affects the national cause.

As players we might be at each other's throats one week, and then pulling on the gold jumper together the next. My point is reinforced by the disturbing amount of foul and dirty play witnessed in this year's [1993] interstate series betweeen NSW and Queensland. If a player needs to be cited then he should be, without any parochial interests being a factor. After all, the Wallabies basically draw their playing numbers from a handful of club sides in Brisbane and Sydney. Queensland and NSW need to be working together for Australia, not for self-interest.

GB: *Italian rugby has lured many of the world's elite players over* *the years and it's no secret the players receive handsome financial rewards. How has it worked in your case?*

ML: Well, I'm employed by the Benetton group, the team's sponsors. I work for them during the week and play on Saturdays. Really it's no different to players in Australia who are employed by sponsors of the various unions. I've been involved in the press department and responsible for the English and American markets, monitoring how the company is perceived through the media. I also look at the economic climates in those countries and the performance of our product.

GB: *How lucrative is it?*

ML: It's very lucrative from both a financial and cultural point of view. I enjoy the cultural side as much as the financial. Remember, I left very good employment in Australia to go to Italy. It was a big decision to make, but one I certainly don't regret.

GB: *There has been a world wide outcry that administrators are asking too much of their players. Do you agree?*

ML: Well, let me answer by way of illustration. Here in Australia we've had the Springbok tour. The unions have formulated a program which will pay expenses and then make badly needed profits. I really don't have an answer here, but the demands being placed on the players are ridiculous.

The NSW and Queensland players in the Australian team had to play the All Blacks and then a State match plus three Tests against the South Africans, all in the space of five weeks! They're not only playing the two hardest and most physically demanding teams in the world, but they have to maintain a level of performance, fitness, health and mental ability over that intense period. No other sportsman in the world gets asked to do that. Yet here we are as amateurs getting asked to do that, and last year was the same. It's too much for the players, especially this year after the Super Ten series, then an interstate series. No wonder players are tired and jaded.

I don't have an answer other than to say our elite players should be playing fewer matches because we simply don't have the depth in Australian rugby. We need to change national focus from Brisbane and Sydney to the rest of Australia. That's where rugby needs to be promoted and developed, to swell our reserves and make teams like Victoria, South Australia and Western Australia more competitive. Australian rugby needs Wallabies from those States.

• •

Almost a century ago, speedy centre Frank 'Badger' Row spearheaded NSW to a hard-fought three-one series win in the intercolonial matches against Queensland of 1899.

That must have truly stuck in the craw of the northerners because 'Badger' was born and bred in what became known as the Sunshine State.

But it seems there were no hard feelings. In the *NSW Rugby Annual*, published the following year, special reference is made to the 'kindness and splendid hospitality afforded by the Queensland Rugby Union' to the visitors.

■ ■

Orange fullback Larry Dwyer has the unique distinction of captaining the Wallabies in their first victory over the All Blacks (16–5) on New Zealand soil.

The celebrated event took place back in 1913 at Lancaster Park and remains the only time in 100 Tests between the two countries in which the opposing skippers both played at fullback.

Three years earlier, Dwyer had also starred in our first win over New Zealand in Australia, but he only managed that feat after overcoming considerable hardships.

His employers, a penny-pinching legal firm in Orange, demanded that Larry work back on the Friday night to compensate them for the time he'd be taking off to play rugby for his country.

As a consequence, he just managed to catch the midnight mail train to Sydney and then walked from Central Station to the SCG.

Thirty thousand fans saw Australia lose the first Test 6–0, but two days later the Wallabies exacted their historic revenge, triumphing 11–0.

No doubt the extra recovery time made all the difference to Larry, who was acclaimed the 'man of the match'.

Sleeping Giants

There's no doubt that New Zealand has been the major beneficiary of South Sea Island rugby. The trickle of Islanders into All Black ranks in the late eighties has become a fast-moving stream in the nineties. Our old enemies across the Tasman were quick to realise how these players could add speed, strength and skill to a core of experienced home-grown players.

IT'S NOW commonplace for talented rugby footballers from Western Samoa, Fiji and Tonga to shift to New Zealand (and to a lesser extent Australia) to further their rugby educations and help realise their representative aspirations at provincial level and beyond. A three-year residential qualifying period is currently in force for players who've represented their country at Test level and then wish to change to another national team.

This 'Islandisation' of our national team has been far less conspicuous than that of our New Zealand neighbours, but apparent nonetheless. Fijian speedster Acura Niuqila made Wallaby ranks in 1988. Then along came Tongan powerhouse Willie Ofahengaue. Next another Fijian, Ilie Tabua, and more recently another powerful Tongan, Daniel Manu. All three made major impacts when introduced to Wallaby colours. Sydney-raised Tongan, Fili Finau, also gained a gold jumper on the tour of France in 1993. Back then I wrote this article on our blossoming South Sea Island connections and the mystique of these new 'quiet men' of Australian rugby.

'If they're not in their rooms they'll be asleep somewhere.' NSW forward John Langford was referring to his two Tongan team-mates Willie Ofahengaue and Fili Finau. The third member of the Wallabies' Pacific islands triangle, Ilie Tabua, also enjoys his slumber. Away from rugby, it seems, their greatest preoccupation is with sleeping. On tour, team-mates say all three would rather have a doze than go sight seeing. Australian coach Bob Dwyer goes a step further. 'They'd rather sleep than do anything else! All three would be the quietest and shyest people I've met.'

So will these 'sleeping giants' ever play together in the Australian back row? The answer, most probably, is yes. 'That was our intention if Willie had been fit for the French tour,' said Dwyer. 'Ilie would be open-side flanker and Fili would play No. 8. They're all such punishing tacklers. The opposition would be terrified.'

Like the Western Samoans (whom Dwyer rates as a big threat in the next World Cup on the hard South African grounds), Willie, Ilie and Fili enjoy putting an opponent on the ground with maximum impact. Willie's ferocious hit on Uli Schmidt at Capetown in last year's one-off international effectively ended the Springboks' second-half challenge. Similarly, Ilie Tabua's debut against the Boks at Ballymore featured a torrent of stupendous defensive hits. Fili maintained the tradition in France.

Willie 'O' and Fili were both born in Tonga and then went to school in New Zealand before finding their way across the Tasman, but in different circumstances. Fili made the passage first when his family decided to settle in Sydney. He finished his schooling at Homebush Boys' High. Willie's plight has been well documented. He starred against Australia with the touring NZ Schoolboys in 1988 but then was refused re-entry to his adopted country because of an invalid visa. His dream of winning the World Cup in an All Black jumper certainly went horribly wrong for the Kiwis.

Ilie 'T' arrived in Brisbane in the mid-1980s from Fiji and has played with three clubs—GPS, Norths and Brothers. Like his countryman Acura Nuiqula, he became a dual International and his memorable performance at Ballymore was 'simply the best'. His man-of-the-match effort so inspired Brothers' first-grade winger Jason 'Rupert' McCall, a best selling sporting poet, that he penned the following verses:

> Look at him go, the human skewer
> Look at him, look at him, Ilie Tabua.
> Look at him running, low to the around
> Look at him hammer, look at him pound.
> Look at him poise, like a heavyweight punch
> Look at him launch, look at him crunch.
> Look at him eying the Wallaby spot
> Look at him smiling, that's what he got.
> Look at him hunting enemy 'Bok
> Armed with shoulders carved out of rock.
> There ain't no stopping the human skewer
> Look at him, look at him, Ilie Tabua.

A broken arm sustained in the First Test in Bordeaux against France prematurely ended Ilie's first Wallaby tour. Ironically, the injury presented his Tongan 'cousin' Fili with a chance in the limelight against the French Baa Baas at Clermont-Ferrand.

'Fili is an outstanding prospect,' says Dwyer. 'You have to

remember he's still a boy. He played for the Australian Under 21s this year. He's going to get bigger and stronger. As a player he's very athletic, very good in the lineout, he runs strongly and is a punishing tackler. At the moment he needs to understand how good he's going to be.'

The Australian coach has been watching Tabua's progress for several seasons. 'Like Fili he's excellent in the lineout but his biggest strength is his tremendous explosive power.' Dwyer pointed out that the turning point in Ilie's fortunes probably came against the All Blacks in 1992 when he was chosen to represent a South Australian President's XV. 'He totally outjumped Mike Brewer, which is no mean feat.'

Sadly, 1993 was a forgettable year on the football field for the inspirational Willie 'O'. He missed the domestic season with a severe knee injury after an off-season playing stint in Italy. Then he caught everyone by surprise, including close friends, when he married. Only the bride's parents knew. (In fact the bride's father, the Reverend at the Manly Uniting Church, carried out the ceremony.)

Therein lies one important key to the trio. They're all deeply religious and in Tonga the church and rugby are closely aligned. The belief is that if you are given a talent you must use it to your fullest. Willie spent much of the 1991 World Cup campaign reading the Bible. Perhaps the commonly held religious faith explains their reserved, level-headed approach to life and rugby.

Chris Hawkins, coach of the Sydney premiers Gordon, also coached the Australian Schoolboys for five years with outstanding success. But he watched his team almost single-handedly demolished by the 'Tongan Torpedo' in the NZ side back in 1988. He also coached Fili on the unbeaten national schoolboy tour to the UK in 1990–91. 'Tongans are very reserved and they are always smiling, but they do have a breaking point,' he says. 'Willie showed that in the World Cup quarter-final against

Ireland when Phil Matthews overstepped the line in the opening seconds. On our tour in 1991, there was a bit of trouble brewing in a nightclub involving some team members and locals. The normally reserved Fili stepped in and the incident was over. He's a big boy and he sorted it out very quickly.' In Finau's case, Hawkins feels that despite his enormous potential, 'he doesn't produce until the word is put on. The more you ask the more he gives. If you need him to 'switch on' in a crisis he'll suddenly jump higher than everyone else and run faster. He has incredible coordination but he needs a strong personality in tune with him, to teach him to play for eighty minutes.'

But whatever their ultimate rugby fortunes in Wallaby colours may hold, these tremendously talented Island players have already been repaying something of a debt. After all, it was Australian teachers and missionaries who introduced rugby in Tonga at the turn of the century.

• •

Who holds the All-England Schools 200 yards low hurdles record at 22.1 seconds?

None other than Gareth Edwards, regarded as one of rugby's greatest scrum-halves. Edwards set that record back in 1965. He left Alan Pascoe—the future Commonwealth and European 400m hurdles champion—trailing a full thirteen metres in his wake.

Gareth displayed that same withering turn of speed for the Barbarians against the All Blacks in 1973, finishing off what many still believe is the greatest try of all time in the Baa Baas' immortal 23–11 showpiece victory.

• •

• •

Llanelli fullback Edward 'Ned' Roberts must have been a pretty practical sort of boyo.

Facing a raging snowstorm one Saturday afternoon, the former Welsh international took the field against Gloucestershire in his overcoat.

Last century most fullbacks spent muchof their time hanging about, but Roberts was renowned for injecting himself into backline movements.

Perhaps those flashing forays were just Ned's way of trying to keep warm?

■ ■

Rob Louw

Doctor Danie Craven has described Rob Louw as 'one of the best Springboks ever to represent South Africa'. The tall, powerful loose forward played nineteen Tests in the early eighties after refining his immense rugby skills at Stellenbosch University. He's been tagged a rebel by many people at home. 'Maybe it was my long hair. Certainly I've never been afraid to speak my mind,' he told me.

Louw always abhorred apartheid and is godfather to Errol Tobias's first son. (On the riot-torn tour of New Zealand in 1981 Tobias became the first non-white South African Springbok.) Then, in 1985 Louw and Springbok three-quarter Ray Mordt switched to rugby league, signing on with glamour English club Wigan for record fees.

I conducted this interview with Louw in Cape Town while on tour with the Wallabies for the historic rematch of the two international rugby giants. He spoke with characteristic frankness about his time as a professional and the volatile relationship between sport and politics in South Africa.

GB: *Having yourself turned professional, what is your current involvement with rugby union?*

RL: The arrival of the All Blacks and the Wallabies is the first contact I've had with rugby since 1985. My energies have been devoted to my boating business. [Rob's thriving company manufactures and exports rubber duckies.]

I can look in from the outside—I had three years in England and we were the first South Africans to turn professional in a long time. Before that I went to Italy and played against Campo—he was first-five [fly-half] with Petrarca. There was big money involved then. The players were paid but there are ways of getting around it. They put me on a company payroll and gave me the works—a car, house and big salary. I think it's a very good thing actually. In rugby league I played against Wally Lewis's Australians and I can tell you there are many players who would go to league tomorrow if it wasn't for Italian rugby.

In South Africa they're trying to get the players completely away from Italian rugby and just play here and I don't believe that's good. Italian rugby is good because the players are being paid fairly well there and that keeps them away from rugby league. The professional code is a major problem for union in Australia and New Zealand, especially New Zealand. Australians and South African rugby union players are fairly well off—they come from more of a middle-class situation—whereas New Zealanders have more of a working-class base. There's a big incentive for them to go across to rugby league and make money.

GB: *How should rugby authorities address the question of professionalism?*

RL: It's a difficult situation. I've played for money and received very good rewards. We 'turned' in 1985 for the second biggest signing ever. Terry Holmes signed up for £80,000. We signed up for £65,000 for a three-year contract. Then on top of that, you had your playing contracts and payments above the lump sum, which in South Africa was five times, about 400,000 Rand ($A200,000) in 1985, which would be worth more than a million now. I was involved in five finals with Wigan, John Player League, that type of contest and in every game we got a big incentive also. So there was quite a bit of money to make. I think the way to go for rugby union is to commercialise the players. It's happening quite a bit now—sponsorship, endorsements, television appearances and so on.

What we don't want is the situation I experienced where five minutes before we ran out for a final, the players were still arguing about money. That's not rugby. I experienced the situation where you play the match and even after a big final you just pick up the money and leave—there's no player contact. That isn't on and that's where the camaraderie of rugby union is so fantastic. Many of the players with Wigan now are former rugby union men. They still dream of going back to rugby. I'm talking about the top ones like Joe Lydon and the like. He's a very good friend of ours and played rugby union for England Under 19s. Many of those guys still think about playing rugby union. Although they've made a lot of money and love playing league, they always remember that friendship and camaraderie which they will never get, unfortunately, in rugby league.

Rugby union has to look forward. Time these days is money. I read about Phil Kearns. He's a great player, but he's away from work for four or five months this year. It's a very difficult situation. I think trust funds are one way to go. They've worked fantastically well in athletics. What happened in the past with South African rugby, and remember it's already fairly professional, is that a player will go from club to club or province to province for money. However, if the club or province set up a trust fund for that player you'd generate loyalty and that's probably the way to go.

Although I turned pro, I'm still fairly conservative but you've got to appreciate that these top players like Campo and Naas Botha only have so many years to make money out of rugby. You've got to keep them happy with incentives, otherwise you'll lose them to rugby league. There's a lot of money out there. I know there was a very big offer made to England's captain, Will Carling, but he declined because of the incentives to stay. Most rugby union players love their set-up—there aren't too many who've turned to league and said that rugby union was, excuse the word, 'bullshit'. As I said before, they'd still love to be back there with the whole camaraderie of the game. When I turned, no South African Springbok had done so, to rugby league, for twenty years because we don't see the game at all. They keep it away from us over here. Then, myself and Ray Mordt turned and I felt I'd really sinned. The press here made us feel as if we were tainted, but not so the rugby union authorities. We were made welcome when we returned home.

GB: *The integration of Blacks and Coloureds—are the authorities going the right way?*

RL: I've always been politically motivated for change. Back in the early eighties Dr Craven would take myself, Ian Kirkpatrick, a black guy and a Coloured guy out into the real outback, the real farming communities. Doc used to walk in and just shock the whole system. He'd say, 'We've got to have a shared community and shared fields'. People will never believe the huge influence Doc Craven has had on the change in our country and it's sport that has brought that change. He's done so much and people would never believe it. The Coloureds and the Moslems are crazy about rugby and they're mainly in the Western Cape and Eastern Province on the Port Elizabeth side.

The Blacks—we have one tribe, the Xhosa, who quite like rugby—but the percentage of them playing is still very small. I remember in 1982 going up to Zululand and trying to get the Zulus to play rugby but it just hasn't taken off with them. They just don't like the physical contact. They're very strong but I don't think rugby, unfortunately, will ever be a major sport with them. They get their physical involvement with boxing and soccer. They love those sports. Athletically they're very talented, they're brilliant, but it seems rugby will always be a poor relation to boxing and soccer for them. They have probably seen quite a bit of rugby but it needs a lot of work and a lot of marketing—a lot of money has already been spent in their community and I'd love to see some success because I think rugby would be very good for the Zulus.

GB: *Is everyone getting the opportunity to play?*

RL: I think we are a bit behind cricket. There's a lot of politicking and a lot of infighting. Unfortunately rugby is being used as a political football. In a political sense the people know that rugby, although soccer is the majority sport, is supported very much by the government and the Afrikaaners so they use rugby that way. The same way as the ANC support soccer.

I was on the 1981 demonstration tour of New Zealand and other demonstration tours so I've seen the whole lot. Where you have times of quick change in any country you will have problems and we are experiencing quick change now. Unfortunately the players are being used because of our system here in the past. We all know how wrong it was.

Back in 1981 the chief opposition white party in South Africa was anti-apartheid. So there has been a very large core of South Africans who haven't liked apartheid, who abhorred it. I was very strongly involved in those days. Errol Tobias and I went through the whole NZ tour together as very close mates. I've always hated apartheid and I've always told people that. Unfortunately, people in Australia and New Zealand haven't realised that there's a large portion of South Africans who've hated apartheid. Errol, incidentally, has done very well for himself. He's a builder out of Cape Town and we keep in close contact. He was a great player. I liken him to the first players to go across to American basketball and baseball in the 1930s and 1940s. In ten years' time he'll be revered as the first black player to move across and play with the white South Africans at the top level.

GB: *The question of who will succeed 'Doc' Craven is a topical issue. Do you think Louis Luyt is the man?*

RL: After what happened at Ellis Park—no. The silence was a sad situation. If they'd told the public they would have the anthem sung beforehand I don't think the crowd would have stood up and sung it. They thought it had been taken away from them completely.

After the Olympic Games in Barcelona where we didn't even have a flag or an anthem, a lot of white South Africans were sitting here saying, what the heck is this all about? South Africa has never had national pride, we've never had a flag. People have never waved flags at games and suddenly there's been a big white national pride coming out and the Coloureds have joined up with whites which is a great thing because it's the first time there's been a bit of a nationality feeling. But it was a bad thing that happened at Ellis Park. It was a very poor show. We've never had problems in Cape

Town. We've always lived very easily with the Blacks and Coloureds. Here it's more liberal. We've mixed with no hassles. It'll be a different story with the rugby crowd in Cape Town. [He was right—twenty seconds of silence was dutifully observed, in lieu of the usual playing of a national anthem.]

Louis Luyt should be held responsible for what happened at Ellis Park. Representing the Transvaal RU he was in control and he should have told the spectators that the national anthem was going to be played. People sang out of spontaneity, thinking it wasn't going to happen. If they had said 'we are playing the anthem', then I think the silence would have been observed. It was a token effort really by those in charge at Ellis Park.

GB: *Who are the alternatives to lead South African rugby?*

RL: There is no white administrator that stands out. Ebrahim Patel—the current co-president—is a great man and I think he can take over the reins. Whether he can get the true hard-liner Afrikaaner to follow him will be another story. But he's the type of guy to do it. He's a good man, he's a Coloured and a Moslem. Unfortunately the Coloureds have been Christian-orientated so that means in-fighting because they could be anti-him. There's no white administrator in my opinion who has the charisma or the strength to take over what 'Doc' Craven has done. Because he's had so many years as president he's left such a giant void and there's nobody really jumping out.

GB: *Is it right that the ANC can hold rugby tours to ransom?*

RL: Well, they're going to be our future. I think they're using rugby as a political football but I think the demands they made for the Tests are fair demands. I feel, though, that the ANC must look at things in perspective. We had the South African national soccer team playing against Cameroon. They also had their call for a minute's silence, but nobody was silent. So it's very difficult but you've got to look at things fairly. As long as the players can rule the game and not the politicians then we can go somewhere. The players feel that same way about their lot. But when the politicians get involved, as they are, then it can get ugly. I hope it doesn't hurt the players.

• •

The 1969 Wallaby team to South Africa were outclassed by their hosts. They lost all four Tests, conceding a lopsided thirteen tries to two.

But the Australians established an unusual record during their twenty-six-game tour by kicking an extraordinary sixteen dropped goals.

Sydney University fly-half Rupert Rosenblum—an acknowledged master of the boot—was the main contributor, notching up a personal tally of eleven.

Unlucky not to be selected for that touring party were future NSWRU president Peter Crittle, and coaching and development supremo, Alec Evans.

The Australians struggled throughout that tour to match the sheer bulk of their opponents. In those days, a dominant pack could almost always be expected to deliver a victory at Test level.

The Wallabies were on the receiving end of some torrid scrummaging, but one young prop who developed well on tour went on to become assistant Wallaby coach—'Jake' Howard.

He didn't get to play in any of the tests, but his impressive work-rate earned him the nickname 'Tractor' from his team-mates.

Phil Kearns

The press often describe him as a baby-faced assassin, but his pet hate is any front rower with tough whiskers. 'I'm not renowned for my facial hair and the Frenchmen in particular have tough whiskers. It's a shocker, they tend to take a bit of skin off my face.'

UNTIL recently Phil Kearns was the outstanding hooker in international rugby. This smiling, cherub-cheeked businessman cum developer has completed his rugby degree in spectacular fashion. From second XV at Newington College to his first Test cap against the New Zealand All Blacks five years later, you could say Kearns has been in rugby's fast lane. Until injury struck, there was no sign of the pace slackening.

In 1992, at just twenty-five, he found himself leading the Wallabies in Ireland and Wales after an injury to Michael Lynagh. In 1995 he captained Australia to a series win over the Springboks, despite losing the first Test.

Australian coach Bob Dwyer had followed Kearns' early development with Randwick's first-grade Colts team and was impressed by his skill and mobility. Tipping the scales at 105 kgs, he was almost too good to be true. In 1988 the young Kearns captained the Australian Under 21 team against the NZ Colts, who suffered the indignation of conceding a pushover try against the old enemy.

The following year, Dwyer plucked Kearns from Randwick's reserve grade side to face the All Blacks in the cauldron of Eden Park in Auckland. Over forty Tests later he's universally revered as one of the best forwards in the game. With Test front-row partners Tony Daly and Ewen McKenzie, the B.A. economics graduate gave the Wallabies a forward platform equal to any in the world.

The bad news for his opponents is that he aims to be around for the 1999 World Cup. (Don't forget Sean Fitzpatrick led the All Blacks at thirty-two years of age in his third World Cup.) But, as the following interview confirms, Phil Kearns' continuing rugby career will always be based on his father Keith's advice: 'Enjoy yourself. If you're not enjoying it don't play it.'

GB: *When do you recall rugby first taking hold of you?*

PK: I played my first game of rugby at the age of seven at Green Reserve, the park next door to where I live at Blakehurst. The Blakehurst Blues asked me to come down and have a run. I scored a try in my first game mainly because I was a bit bigger than the other kids and the staple move tended to be 'Kearnsy on the Burst'. There haven't been too many follow-up tries since then but I guess that moment ignited the spark.

GB: *Was it a personal blow only making the second XV rugby team at Newington College?*

PK: Yes it was. I made the first XV for the opening game of the season. That was special because all the footie teams at Newington wear black except for the first XV who wear white. But I was dropped for the next game and had to hand my white jumper back, which was devastating because so much emphasis was placed on being in the top team. The following year I went to Randwick to try out as hooker for their Colts teams. I remember Mum saying, 'Don't be disappointed if you only make fourth grade.' I still rib her about that huge vote of confidence. I ended up playing first-grade Colts for two years and that's where the seed was planted because I said to myself, 'Maybe I can go all right at this game.' There was a little bit of extra satisfaction because one of the hookers I beat for the first-grade spot in the Colts had played for the Australian Schoolboys the previous year, when I'd been playing in the seconds at Newington.

GB: *What were your other sporting interests as a child?*

PK: As a kid I played everything, actually. I tried T-ball, baseball, soccer for a little while and I was captain of swimming at Newington. I was a freestyle sprinter—long distance isn't my go. I trained in a swim squad from the age of six right through to twelve or thirteen, then took it up again from fifteen to the end of school. I've just taken it up again recently and am thoroughly enjoying it. It's also helped enormously in my recovery from last season's Achilles tendon problem.

GB: *Could you give an insight into the stress on your body packing into scrum after scrum, at the highest level?*

PK: I think there are probably a few other things more stressful. You just have to look at the sizes of the packs of forwards you're playing against. Last year the three front rowers in the French pack were over 110 kgs. The two second rowers were 125 kgs plus, and the three back rowers were all between 115 and 120. The Australian pack is a similar weight, maybe a touch lighter and I'm stuck in the middle of all of this. One side is trying to push my head out my backside and the other's trying to push my backside out of my head. So it is fairly stressful and I can assure you I have great trouble getting out of bed the morning after a Test match.

GB: *What about the crashing together of two such monster packs at the scrum engagement?*

PK: Usually myself and the tighthead take the brunt of the impact, because we're the first ones to get hit. It's like trucks hitting each other and my shoulders are certainly starting to feel it. Both AC shoulder joints have been hit hard. I've torn both ligaments and the left one has snapped away so it can't get any worse. The right one's halfway there. I expect I'll have ceramic joints by the time I'm forty. You have to be a masochist really. Although I may feel like a cripple for two days, I enjoy the contact, especially if it's against good opponents—and you win.

GB: *What was it like playing your first Test match, which happened to be against the All Blacks?*

PK: I was rooming with Simon Poidevin who'd been playing against the All Blacks since 1980. That was a memorable experience. I walked in after training one day and he was sitting there with a priest on the bed apparently counselling him. I thought, 'Shit, what have I got myself into here, the Last Rites?' I remember the training sessions and the lineout jumpers going crook about my throw-ins. Nothing's changed. I also remember Sean Fitzpatrick, the All Black hooker, giving me a mouthful and doing a lot of talking. Things like 'You're only a kid, what do you think you're doing on the field against the best team in the world? Get off the field, little boy'. I tried not to take any notice, but it stuck. I also remember losing and being totally devastated.

GB: *Is that why you gave Fitzpatrick two fingers and a verbal when you scored the match-winning try in the third Test in Wellington the following year?*

PK: You could say it was a release of some pent-up emotion. I was inviting him around for a barbecue. I originally thought of one barbecue and then put two fingers up suggesting he come around for a second. Truthfully, what I really said in the heat of that moment couldn't be repeated in any publication.

GB: *Before your first Test, you asked me to give a cheerio in the commentary to your cheer squad back in Sydney—the Gong Beaters in Baz's bombshelter and Chad. Who are they?*

PK: They're basically a bunch of guys that I went to school with. We went on a tour to the USA and Canada in 1987 and for some reason we started calling ourselves the 'Gong Beaters'. The guys were watching that test at Baz's place, a bit like a granny flat which he called his bombshelter. Chad was a mate of mine who lives out in the bush now and whenever he invites friends over he always replays the video saying, 'Watch this, I'm famous!' They're just a great bunch of school friends who I've always kept in contact with. Some of them still play rugby, including Scott Barker who plays first grade for Randwick.

GB: *Who is your toughest and most respected opponent?*

PK: Definitely Sean Fitzpatrick. I've played against him about fifteen times for NSW and Australia. So far I haven't come up against a hooker who's as quick around the field, as tough, or probably even as dirty as him. They're all facets of his game and I'd like to think we have a healthy mutual respect. It may sound a bit conceited but when you've got two guys who have been rivals in two of the world's best XVs over the past few years, although we are friendly, we don't like to be over-friendly.

GB: *If I asked your wife, Julie, to describe the sort of person you are, how would you expect her to reply?*

PK: [*laughs*] Gee, I don't know. There must be a few good things, otherwise she wouldn't have married with me, I guess. As far as my rugby is concerned she'd definitely say I was hardworking. She'd probably tell you I hate losing. Even when we play backgammon or pool against each other, I'm filthy if I lose, there's no doubt about that. I'm punctual as I can be but sometimes I'm a little late. My father always told me to be on time. I think I'm reasonably kind and fairly considerate and generous, I guess. I try to be generous with my time with her and the things we do together.

GB: *What has been the most exhilarating game you've ever played in?*

PK: Definitely Australia versus France at Ballymore in 1990. We won 48–31. It stands out as the most spectacular and most exhilarating. There was so much ball movement and I remember feeling as tired as I've ever been. The day was unusually hot and we got away to a dream start leading 18–0 after eighteen minutes. It was one of those Tests that goes by really quickly. You don't think how tired you are even though your legs are starting to tighten up and get heavy. I'll never forget Serge Blanco's 100-metre try in that game. He offered Campo a dummy when he got to halfway and then outsprinted Campo, Ian Williams and Paul Carozza for the second fifty metres. I just watched in awe.

GB: *What about the worst match you've played in?*

PK: Australia and New Zealand in Auckland before the last World Cup. We lost 6–3. It was by far the worst game I've played in. The game was a bore, and the refereeing was disgraceful with non-stop whistle throughout. In hindsight, though, it was a very good motivational tool for our World Cup semi-final clash against NZ later that year at Lansdowne Road in Dublin.

GB: *Can you relate your most embarrassing moment on a rugby pitch?*

PK: It was a shocker. I was playing in an invitation game with Murray Mexted [the former All Black No. 8] over in Wellington and we were winning very easily. A couple of team-mates then said, 'Kearnsey, why don't you have a shot at goal?' There was quite a large crowd, probably about 5000, and I've lined the ball up to take the shot, stepped back five paces, all set. However the loop in one of my shoelaces was a bit long and it caught the stud of my other boot as I stepped into the approach. I fell flat on my face. All of the opposition have run up and charged, picked the ball up and continued playing while I'm lying on the ground in fits of laughter along with the rest of the crowd.

GB: *How did you enjoy the captaincy of Australia and the NSW Waratahs?*

PK: I loved it. The South African series in 1993 was particularly memorable for me. I'd led Australia to a loss against the All Blacks in Dunedin and then lost the first Test to the Springboks. I thought I was going to be the Kim Hughes of Australian rugby. We had terrific spirit in the team and it was a huge thrill to fight back and win that series against South Africa.

GB: *How would you describe your captaincy style?*

PK: It differs from game to game. I try to sense what the mood in the team is, whether they want me to talk a fair bit. I try not to talk too much and try and have all the guys involved in the decisions. If we're scrummaging I want everyone to have an input. I guess it's consensus captaincy in a way.

GB: *How do you relax away from rugby?*

PK: I generally like keeping fit so I spend a fair bit of time at the gym or pool. I love playing golf, I also love surfing and snow skiing. However I get very little time to do those sorts of things. My golf handicap is a joke. It's about twenty-two at the moment but I have had it as low as seventeen when I was at university playing two or three times per week. Unfortunately at the moment it's blowing out further all the time.

GB: *What is the special mystique about the front rowers' club?*

PK: Hard to say, but I guess it's because we're much more intelligent than any other positions. If you want some decent conversation you talk to the front rowers. The backs are talking about girls and that sort of stuff all the time while the front rowers are more concerned about political issues and the state of the world. I guess we're just more interesting to hang round and we appreciate each other's company more than anyone else.

The Taranaki Pig Farmer

Much of rugby's unique character stems from the characters who play the game, be they anonymous sub-district stalwarts or Test match superstars. New Zealand is famous for producing tough-as-teak farmers who climb down from their tractors on Saturdays to play inspired football. Many of them are truly the stuff of legend.

WHAT ON EARTH is going on? My eyes must be playing tricks on me. Here are the mighty All Blacks—the demi-gods of international rugby—preparing for the deciding Test of the 1980 Bledisloe Cup series against Australia and . . . (look again) . . . they're passing *house bricks* to each other?

Was this really happening? When I was a youngster my father used to tell me about the mystique and power of those 'men in black'. I'd heard all those stories about Colin Meads charging up hillsides on his farm with a sheep on his back. But never, never, had I seen anything like this.

It was, in fact, a 'closed' training session that day at St John's Oval in the grounds of Sydney University. Even the students, criss-crossing the College playing fields between lectures, stopped in their tracks to watch. I presumed it was some new form of

Spartan exercise whose meaning was a secret confined to the 'chosen few' of the All Blacks.

And, at least for me, it remained an intriguing secret for the next fifteen years. So, when the opportunity cropped up during a 1995 trip to New Zealand to finally solve The Great House Brick Mystery, I leapt at it.

Picture the scene: a sparkling winter's day in New Zealand's spectacular North Island. Snow-capped Mt Taranaki formed a breathtaking background to some of the finest farming country in the world. Following directions, I drove through Inglewood and ten minutes out of town took a careful left turn into Rugby Road. There, three houses down, the residence of the legendary Taranaki Pig Farmer himself, Dave 'Trapper' Loveridge.

The former scrum-half was captain of those 1980 All Blacks. That series against the Wallabies has a special place in my memory because it was my first as a television rugby commentator. To mark the occasion I'd worked hard to coin a few distinctive nicknames for some of the New Zealanders. Loveridge became 'The Taranaki Pig Farmer', Mark 'Cowboy' Shaw was 'The Manawatu Meatworker'. My beginner's ploy must have struck a chord with Australian rugby viewers because even today I'm still frequently asked, 'Hey, Gordon—how's the Taranaki Pig Farmer'?

But back to those house bricks. What was the real story? Settling in for what became a splendid session of rugby yarnspinning, Dave Loveridge was happy to reveal all.

'We'd dropped a few balls in the previous game,' he told me. 'So our physio, Malcolm Hood, thought that the backs should pass a house brick. It was really a bit of fun. His reasoning was that if we dropped the brick it would land on our feet. We got cleaned out in the Test so I guess you could say it backfired.'

Dave Loveridge played twenty-four Internationals for New Zealand between 1979 and 1985. He holds pride of place in New Zealand's rollcall of outstanding scrum-halves. A brilliant passer and kicker, Loveridge was also a penetrating runner from the scrum base. In the style later exemplified by Nick Farr-Jones, he had that crucial ability to control the course of a match. After the first International against the Lions in 1983 in Wellington, All Black coach Bryce Rope commented on Loveridge's contribution: 'That is the finest display I have seen from any halfback in any game anywhere in the world.'

The 'Trapper's' Test debut at Cardiff Arms Park in 1978 was infamous for Andy Haden's last-minute lineout 'dive' which saw Wales penalised and then pipped 13–12 by the resulting kick at goal by Brian McKechnie. Again I pressed Dave for the inside story.

'The real story is that Andy was suffering from middle-ear infection and lost his balance and fell out. Actually I didn't see the incident at all. I was too busy watching the ball although I felt the breeze as his huge frame came crashing to the ground beside me.'

(Although the Welsh claimed they were robbed, referee Roger Quittenton later revealed that Haden's action had nothing to do with the penalty. He'd actually penalised Geoff Wheel, who was two places ahead of Haden in the lineout, for jumping off the shoulder of his opponent.)

The 1981 series against the Springboks in New Zealand remains an uneasy memory for 'Trapper'. It was an experience he wouldn't wish to go through again.

'All I could see at one point was a plane coming over the top of a lineout and then the flour bombs. The first two Tests were fiercely competitive but that decider at Eden Park wasn't enjoyable because of the circumstances. It was great to be playing against a team of the Springboks' calibre but it was certainly an era I'll never forget.'

The Taranaki Pig Farmer watched the emergence of modern Australian rugby first-hand. He was on the reserves' bench ('thankfully') at Eden Park in 1978 when Greg Cornelsen scored his four tries against the All Blacks in what remains the highest Test score ever conceded by New Zealand . . . 30–16.

In 1980 Loveridge witnessed the phenomenal talents of Mark Ella as a rookie Wallaby fly-half. Being the losing captain in that series was not exactly enjoyable for Dave, who concedes the future Australian captain made life extremely difficult for his opponents on the playing field.

'He was a genius with the ball. One of the greatest first-fives in the game's history, really. The pity of it was that he retired so early. His skill level was of the highest standard but the bugger was also unpredictable. He regularly pulled these magical things out of the box to turn and win games.

'He was just such a gifted player, and then when you had the three of them together, you really didn't know what to expect. Mark was unorthodox and instinctive and that's why we found him such a difficult opponent.'

But in the Test era which followed, rugby fans were never to see the dream contest between two truly great scrum-halves, Nick Farr-Jones and 'The Trapper'.

'I never played a Test match against Nick. He was just coming into his prime when I was on the way out,' Loveridge recalled. 'However, I did play a few Barbarian games against him and actually shared a room with him in Britain in 1986 for the IRB [International Rugby Board] Centenary match between the northern and southern hemispheres. We had a great time teaming up with you Aussies and the South Africans. I remember Mark Shaw one night, leaning on the bar with a concerned look on his face. Simon Poidevin walked up and asked what was wrong. Cowboy replied, "I'm bloody worried, mate, I'm beginning to like you bastards"!'.

The Farr-Jones/Michael Lynagh era epitomised the strength of Australian rugby, according to Loveridge. Both had that special ability to control a game. The need to develop a true on-field 'general' now poses special concerns for the Wallabies as they begin their rebuilding program for the 1999 World Cup. But the former Kiwi captain believes that newcomer George Gregan has the ability to reach rugby's ultimate heights.

'I was watching Australia's test against Western Samoa last year with my old All Black buddy Stu Wilson. When he walked through the door I said, 'Hey, come and have a look at this new Aussie halfback. He's not too bad.' I think he's gone on to prove that. He's certainly got a few good qualities.'

To my mind Gregan seemed to suffer behind an under-performing Australian forward pack in the 1995 World Cup. Many critics—and even Wallaby supporters—were quick to write him off. In that light, Loveridge's comments on Gregan deserve consideration.

'He's got a good pass, he covers very well and I think the further the game goes and the more experience he gets, he'll learn to start controlling games when called on to do so. That comes with experience and confidence. He certainly has all the attributes.'

Speed of pass was a hallmark of 'Trapper' Loveridge's game. It's a skill that Gregan himself acknowledges has demanded continuing attention.

'It's not necessarily the length of pass but the *speed* of pass that's important,' says Loveridge. 'The speed of the ball through the hands is critical. Any budding scrum-half has got to eliminate backswing and any other action that is going to slow the ball down. When you think about it, if a guy can run 100 metres in ten seconds, and you slow your pass down by even a fraction of a second, you're talking about metres when it gets out to the wings. It's all about moving the ball as quickly as you can. A good halfback is balanced when he passes. Positioning of your feet is crucial.'

Dave Loveridge is living proof of the adage that a rugby player won't grow old so long as he just keeps playing the game. Together with his wife Jan, he makes the annual trip to Bermuda as a member of the All Blacks Classic team. His youngest son, Andrew, is a promising halfback, while number one son Matthew plays (wait for it) front row! He was already bigger than his Dad at the age of seventeen. His daughter Jonelle is a keen basketballer and also plays touch football.

The affable Kiwi is now a successful businessman who cheerfully acknowledges his huge debt to rugby. He donated all of his international jerseys to the local Inglewood Rugby Club. His portrait in All Black strip immediately commands your attention when you enter the clubhouse. 'Trapper' also contributes expert commentary for the local radio station.

'It's the lasting friendships that make the game so special. Rugby was my passport and we have friends all over the world. I just hope that the code can retain all of its special qualities such as unity and tradition. With the game now going professional, a lot of the fun and enjoyment will disappear at the elite level, because it becomes a job. That's a pity, but time will pass you by if you stand still.'

Considering their relatively small populations, both Australia and New Zealand have enjoyed incredible success on the world's rugby pitches. It's hardly surprising then that it's the Wallaby v All Black encounters which stir our blood like no others.

To say that competition between the two countries is 'intense' is an understatement of considerable magnitude. Let's leave the last word to Dave Loveridge, the Taranaki Pig Farmer:

'I think it's very healthy. We're fierce rivals but I also believe we're pretty good mates off the paddock as well, and that's important.'

And so say all of us.

Greg Smith

After lifting Eastern Suburbs back to first division in the Sydney club premiership competition, coach Greg Smith didn't mark time. He then took the Tricolours to successive first-grade grand finals but, each time, the Galloping Greens from Randwick proved his nemesis. In 1992 his first serious tilt at representative coaching in charge of Sydney produced a startling victory over the All Blacks. Sydney's total of forty points is the highest winning score ever registered against the Kiwis.

GREG SMITH succeeded Bob Dwyer as national coach in controversial circumstances in 1996. As usual, the Queenslanders claimed it had been yet another 'inside job' by NSW. After three years as Waratah coach Smith had the all-important ARU Council numbers over luckless Reds coach, John Connolly. It was yet another blow for Connolly supporters, who claimed his outstanding record with Queensland for almost a decade should have earned him the job. For his part, Dwyer felt he deserved to retain the post to guide the Wallabies through the early stages of professionalism.

In reality it was time for a change. It's also no secret that Smith and Connolly don't like each other. The current Australian mentor is critical of what he perceives as an often negative approach from the Reds in interstate clashes.

Back in 1993, after his first season at the helm of the Waratahs, I sat down with the then high-school teacher to reflect on a difficult campaign which had produced a narrow win over the Springboks, but no joy in State of the Union clashes against the arch enemy.

GB: *What are your reflections on your first season as coach of the Waratahs?*

GS: It was a very difficult year. We had a situation where we had to rebuild the NSW team. There were thirteen players who represented NSW in 1992 who weren't available this year and most of those players were Internationals. Some were overseas, some like Poidevin and Farr-Jones had just retired, plus we'd lost Tombs and Allen, Jorgensen and Willie 'O' were injured. My biggest difficulty was that I'd seen players in grade football but I had no point of reference at representative level. We were blooding people in a very demanding competition like the Super Ten. Some didn't come up to scratch and we found ourselves constantly in the dilemma: do we persevere or give someone else a go? I found the exercise very difficult because there was no established team to work with. In the end we picked a team we were very happy with and it performed well against South Africa. I was extremely disappointed with the games against Queensland. The first contest at Waratah Stadium was close but the second game was most unsatisfactory from my point of view.

I thought the first game was a disgrace. My experience has been that a good game of rugby happens because both teams are trying to play well. When you've got people committing professional fouls all the time and slowing the game up, collapsing scrums and putting pressure on referees, it basically just becomes a shambles. I don't know what a selector would get out of a game like that. Queensland won because a ball hit the upright and bounced straight into the arms of Wilson, and they scored a late try. In the second game Queensland were able to absorb a lot of pressure in the first twenty minutes of the game. Once again we were unable to convert the professional fouls they committed. We received a lot of penalties in that time and were right on top, but then they were able to score a couple of easy tries and in the end they deserved the representation they got for the Dunedin Test.

I wonder, though, about the whole situation. It's difficult for the national selectors because I tend to think that some of those Queensland players play their best football for Queensland and I'm not sure they can reproduce it at a higher level. I don't know why, but it's to the credit of coach John Connolly and their set-up that they really put it on the line for Queensland against NSW. But funnily enough their record overall wasn't that good. I think both unions have a responsibility. We've obviously got to think of our State and pushing the claims of our players for higher honours, but we also have a responsibility to market the game. I just don't think people are interested in watching games like the first one trotted out by NSW and Queensland. It was just a complete farce, but I can assure you from our point of view that wasn't the scenario we intended. I was very disappointed and if a side goes out with negative tactics in mind then there's probably some other game they can get involved with.

GB: *Are you happy with the Super Ten concept?*

GS: I think it's a very positive step. From the players' point of view a lot more people get international experience. It's a wonderful thing for them to be able to travel and play against provinces in other parts of the world. The game against Northern Transvaal at Loftus Versfeld was an unforgettable experience for many of the team. Although we were beaten, many of the blokes will treasure it for the rest of their lives. It definitely helps create a second, third and even fourth tier of players who can come through at international level. In the past it's been simply NSW and Queensland and it's quite amazing to think we won a World Cup with basically thirty players on show.

I was very pleased with the rise of Scott Bowen. He took his chance when Tim Wallace was injured in the game against Transvaal. I was also pleased with Michael Brial's progress during the season, although I thought he had a bit of a dip in the second interstate game. Warwick Waugh definitely played better football this year than he did in 1992. I think a lot of that had to do with the fact that he wasn't burdened with the responsibility of jumping at four for NSW. He jumped at two on our throw and I thought he competed well and I actually thought he played very well in the first Test against the Springboks. Matthew Burke played well at outside centre, particularly against Transvaal and South Africa.

Semi Taupeaafe played well and Peter Jorgensen came back wonderfully from his injury. When you look at it, John Langford had a marvellous season. Considering the amount of top-level football he's had, he did a great job for the Waratahs because he was one of the really inexperienced players we had to rely on continually. And I think one of the players who really developed during the season was hooker Mark Bell. He was a terrific team man and a great trainer. My advice to him was to study the top hookers like Kearns, Fitzpatrick and Schmidt, who are impact players.

After his retirement the mercurial Mark Ella successfully turned his hand to TV commentary with ABC Sport. *Photo: ABC Document Archives*

The ABC rugby commentary team in the mid eighties. Wallaby great Trevor Allan had taken over from Cyril Towers in the early seventies as the expert commentator. *Photo: ABC Document Archives*

'The Good, the Bad and the Ugly' in no particular order. Messrs Gary Pearse, Chris Handy and Gordon Bray rug up for a big call at Eden Park, Auckland.

Wallaby hero Tim Gavin in action against the 1991 English tourists.
Five years later he prepared on a diet of Iranian caviar and French
cognac. *Photo: Action Photographics*

Brilliant Queensland centre Jason Little in full cry during the dramatic 1991 World Cup quarter-final against Ireland. *Photo: Action
Photographics*

The crowning glory. Wallaby skipper Nick Farr-Jones accepts the Webb Ellis Cup from Her Royal Highness. By the Queen's side is I.R.B. President Roger Vanderfield who refereed the 1965 Waratah Shield final. *Photo: Action Photographics*

The famous bathtubs at Twickenham. 'We fill them with boiling water two hours before kick-off to a level of 9-12 inches'. *Photo: Action Photographics*

The triumphant homecoming after the 1991 World Cup. Wallaby legends Phil Kearns and David Campese bask in the glory with a young fan. *Photo: Action Photographics*

'Reach out and touch...' Former head of ABC TV Sport, David Salter, savours the Holy Grail with the Brays at the World Cup Welcome Home dinner in 1991.

Esala Teleni's all conquering Fijian Army team in action at the 1993 Malaysian Tens in Kuala Lumpur.

Hallelujah! A scene the great Australian rugby public never wit-
nessed: the 1993 Wallabies in France on stage at the Lido in Paris.
The excursion was most graciously hosted by Sydney businessman
Paul Ramsay (centre middle).

Down on the farm at Rugby Road, Inglewood. Former All Black scrum-half and skipper Dave Loveridge — 'The Taranaki Pig Farmer'.

Rugby memorabilia — a passionate and rewarding hobby. That's Jean-Pierre from the 1924 Paris Olympics at side left. *Photo: Antiques & Collectibles*

He's been trying to add another dimension to his game and I believe he achieved that during the finals series.

GB: *A marvellous victory over the Springboks. Tell us how you turned things around.*

GS: After the interstate series the disappointment of the players was obvious. Jeff Sayle and the rest of the management were so upset because it really wasn't a reflection of all the hard work put in by the players. The effort and commitment from the whole squad was just fantastic. I think we blundered tactically and I take full responsibility. At the start of the season I thought a mauling game was essential as the opposition weren't committing themselves to the ruck and maul.

We freed things up a lot for the Springbok game. We completely changed the way we played and were fortunate to have a player like Farr-Jones there assisting Phil Kearns in the on-field organisation. And a player like Campese was able to initiate things and show tremendous leadership, a luxury we didn't have throughout the season. Our approach was for quick delivery of the ball with people hitting the tackle line hard rather than the slow mauling game we'd been playing. Full credit though to the South Africans. They allowed us to play that way because of the way they approached the game. They were committed to an attacking game but I think one of the mistakes they made was leaving those two halves [Van der Westhuizen and Le Roux] out of the Test team because they were real impact players, ones who could score points.

GB: *Looking forward to next season, what are your expectations?*

GS: Well, I now feel a lot more comfortable about the situation, because although there will be a lot of players missing we now have an established team. Essentially it's a very good team. There are gaps that have to be filled—for example Warwick Waugh is going to Italy and that's a very big loss to the team—but it's up to us to make sure we fill that gap. We definitely have the personnel to beat Queensland but it's critical that we're ready for the first Super Ten game. Obviously a tour for a squad of thirty beforehand would be the ideal situation.

• •

He's hardly a household name, but Australian rugby supporters owe a huge debt of gratitude to Leonard Brown. A Queenslander educated at Brisbane Grammar, Brown studied medicine at Oxford as a Rhodes Scholar. He played at prop and was capped 18 times for England. During WWI the good doctor attained the rank of Lt Colonel and in 1917 was awarded the Military Cross for bravery. Later, as a member of the International Rugby Board, Brown was instrumental in obtaining IB status for Australia, New Zealand and South Africa. He also assisted in the foundation of the ARFU in 1949.

'Le Gunfighter'

Violent tactics on the rugby pitch can never be tolerated, but I must confess to having a soft spot for one very aggressive Australian front rower by the name of Steve Finnane. He was known quite simply as 'Butcher' to friends, although with their admirable flair the French press in 1976 invented a new tag for him: 'Le Gunfighter'.

STEVE FINNANE tended to play a 'minder' role in Australian teams and his special skills were usually only called upon when the opposition had resorted to street-fighting tactics—as was sometimes the case during that French tour. Three opposition forwards were knocked unconscious by his wicked short uppercut. But on each occasion 'Le Gunfighter' had retaliated after foul play.

The most vivid incident occurred at Narbonne in the south of France. The Wallabies were being repeatedly 'eye-gouged' in the scrums and one particularly stupid prop then had the far-from-bright idea of tampering with Steve's genital area in a most unfriendly manner. At the very next lineout the same player's feet left the ground—probably for the first time in his career—

but not by his own volition. He rocketed skywards and then hit the deck like a proverbial sack of spuds. Finnane had extracted his revenge.

The irate referee, Monsieur Touffrou (who spoke no English) grabbed Steve by the collar and dragged him twenty-five metres to the centre of the field. He then proceeded to remonstrate with him for a clear thirty seconds amid jeers and whistling from the crowd. Then came one of the strangest scenes I have ever witnessed on a rugby field. 'Butcher' started energetically wagging his finger right back at Touffrou. 'Monsieur Arbitre' then pulled the rugged prop back to the place of incident—and awarded a penalty to Australia! By now in an apparent state of panic, it took the referee another ten seconds to reverse the penalty. It was clearly the reaction of a frightened man. (To this day, Steve denies he'd carefully memorised a special French phrase relating to a rather physical form of recrimination.)

Nevertheless, the French Selection went on to win 15–13 after being favoured by a penalty count of 23–3. The same referee had caned the 1971 Wallabies by 19–1.

Australian captain Geoff 'Bunter' Shaw relieved the tension that night with his masterly speech at the post-match dinner. 'And finally, a word for the referee, Monsieur Touffrou. May I simply say you are the best referee we have ever played against!' The appreciative Touffrou stood up and bowed deeply amid cheering and raucous laughter from both teams.

For some unfathomable reason, Finnane used to continually sing a song on tour about sparrows which went something like: 'Sparrows may come and sparrows may go, but don't chase those sparrows away.' I'm sure it was all very meaningful and prophetic but chose not to enquire. My most enduring memory of Steve Finnane on that tour was the image of him stepping onto the bus each day, his walrus moustache drooping snugly beneath a red beret, an apple in his left hand and a copy of *Playboy* tucked into his left armpit. 'Le Gunfighter' even wore that red beret when acting as touch judge in the second International against France at Parc Des Princes.

• •

'This is the happiest day of my life.'

Prudent males reserve that declaration for their wedding day, or the birth of their first child. But there was no such display of decorum or tact from 1963 Wallaby manager Bill McLaughlin. He saved the line for the end of an epic rugby match.

The Australians had just broken the Springbok's remarkable sixteen-Test winning streak by defeating the South Africans 9–5 in the second International at Newlands.

That victory squared the series 1–1. The Wallabies went on to win the third Test in Johannesburg (11–9) before going down in the fourth at Port Elizabeth (22–6).

The stars of the historic Cape Town win were Ken Catchpole and the late Greg Davis. 'Catchy' dictated play in characteristic style from scrum-half, while Davis unnerved the Springbok inside backs with his unrelenting 'blue heeler' attitude.

By the end of the game, coach Alan Roper, a former bomber pilot, was so overcome (some might say 'tired and emotional') that he missed the team transport back to Seapoint.

▪ ▪

Idle curiosity once prompted me to ask Mark Ella: 'What was the hardest game you ever played?'

'Easy!' he replied. 'My first interstate clash with Queensland in Sydney. Mark Loane and Tony Shaw just kept coming at me for the whole game.'

Now that was real intensity. There seems to be a special brand of fervour the Reds bottle and save up for their annual battles against the Blues. To be fair, the Waratahs have themselves generated plenty of self-styled 'passion' of late, but for a Queenslander to pull on that red jumper against the arch enemy is apparently a unique experience.

Centre three-quarter Richard Tombs, a later NSW representative, can claim the rare distinction of having played for both sides. His first State of the Union match was for Queensland in 1988 at Waratah Stadium. Wily coach Bob Templeton chose the fanatical Queensland patriot Peter Grigg to be Tombs's room-mate.

It was a day Tombs remembers only too well.

'On the morning of the game Griggy was so fired up I thought he was going to start warming up on me! It was all aimed at those '#?@!*&! cockroaches and any other name he could come up with. I was mentally exhausted by the time I ran out onto the field.'

But it was all to no avail. As the afternoon unfolded, the Waratahs bolted home 37–15. Perhaps super-psyched Griggy had played his clash before the kick-off.

Ian Williams, the opposing winger, ran in four tries. Not bad for a mere cockroach.

Bob Dwyer

Bob Dwyer's second stint as Wallaby coach from 1988–95 peaked in the middle of his reign. The World Cup triumph in 1991 was the obvious highpoint.

The series win over New Zealand followed by victory over the Springboks less than twelve months later in Cape Town reaffirmed our status as the World's premier rugby nation—and Bob's rating as the number one coach. But two years later cracks began to appear.

IN 1993 a mediocre performance against the All Blacks in Dunedin was followed by a first-up loss to the Springboks in the three-Test home series. Ultimately, the class and experience of Bob Dwyer's squad pulled them through, but there were definite indications that the winning edge was beginning to dull. When you've claimed the summit, there's only one way to go. By his own admission Dwyer was sometimes finding it a real struggle to keep his charges fully motivated. The year-long absence of the brilliant John Eales with a shoulder injury threw additional pressure on the Australian team. Inconsistency became their unwanted companion.

During the end-of-season tour of France that year, the

Wallabies dropped the first test in Cleremont-Ferrand before bouncing back to square the series with an emphatic victory in Paris. Now just eighteen months away from the third World Cup, the defending champions were looking decidedly shaky. But there was always the feeling that the Wallabies would rise to the big occasion when the chips were really down.

I recorded this interview with Dwyer on the eve of Australia's departure for France back in 1993. With the benefit of hindsight, it makes fascinating reading.

GB: *It took the All Blacks two Test matches before they hit their straps against the Lions. In the Wallabies' case it took three, until the second Test against the Springboks, to find their feet. Is there a parallel in the respective performances?*

BD: Well I suppose so. New Zealand performed indifferently in the first two Tests against the Lions and then came good with a vengeance. We started with the easier Test against Tonga, which was fine, but the difficult Test in Dunedin against New Zealand was beyond us. We knew we'd be under-prepared in teamwork and focus and in terms of the style of play we wanted at national level. However, we were confident we could overcome those problems and come up with a win. As it turned out we didn't go anywhere near it. I think it's accurate to say we should have been better prepared and should have had more time together—some off-season sessions and some squad work during the season. It's quite difficult with the very heavy program both NSW and Queensland had, to get the squad together. So to answer your question, yes, there is a parallel.

GB: *Now that the dust has settled, what are your reflections on the Springbok series?*

BD: The South Africans were a much improved side from

last year. The inclusion of some new players and, in most instances, younger ones, provided them with more pace and we thought they were a very quick team all round the paddock. They were quick out wide but also had pace in their back-row forwards and their halves. It took a couple of good performances from us, especially in the second Test and to a large degree in the third, to hold them out. Some of the criticism they've received since arriving home is ill-informed. We thought they were a very good side, well prepared and very well coached.

In terms of Australian rugby it signalled a turnaround in our performances. It seems to me, and I hope I'm not mistaken, that we haven't played all that well since 1991. We played OK last year, certainly not fantastically well, and in 1993 we hadn't played well until the Ballymore Test. The last two Tests against the Springboks are the basis of some improved play from us. I was definitely encouraged and could see we can start to play well again.

GB: *You continued to be a vehement critic of the new ruck/maul law. Any change of heart?*

BD: I still don't like the law. I know there are ways you can play within the law and gain maximum advantage from it, but I still think it creates an unstructured game which I don't like. It creates more kicking, which I'd rather not see. I've always said the teams that were going to suffer most under the new laws were England and Australia, because they played the most structured and controlled game. Structured and controlled doesn't mean don't run the ball or don't kick the ball. It means play with a purpose. You can play a fifteen-man game under the old laws as Australia did in 1991. At the same time you can play a ten or nine-man game under the old laws, which England did. But England realised, as we saw in the World Cup final, that it was never going to be enough to make them ultimately successful, and hence they changed their game.

I think most people realised by the end of 1991 that under the old laws, unless your approach encompassed all aspects of the game, both forwards and backs and in close and out wide, then you weren't going to be in the money. The new laws have tried to force people into playing an expansive game, but from my observation all that's been forced is a predominance of kicking. I would like the law-makers to go back to where we were, the team going forward gets the scrum feed. There is an advantage to be gained, if you want to use it from phase play, by releasing it early, but there are also some advantages to be gained from staying tight and driving in close. Maybe if they could come up with a law that rewards the team running with the ball, that would be useful. You're now penalised for not using the ball from phase play. Maybe if they rewarded people for using it you'd achieve better results.

GB: *National coaches and panel representatives from most of the major rugby nations met during the Hong Kong Sevens to discuss the laws. Should this be the way for the future?*

BD: It was a very positive meeting, although the coaches were very wary of giving vent to their full feelings because they thought it had no chance of success through the IRB. Now that in itself is an indictment. The national coaches should be able to meet, confident that if they speak their mind to the fullest extent, their thoughts will be noted by the law-makers. The coaches are the people charged with the responsibility and accountability for playing the game, and generally are the most experienced. Therefore it would seem a waste if they don't use them. The contributions made by all the coaches were terrific. There was no evidence of any ego, just a desire to improve the game as the coaches saw it. They are going to be right more often than they are wrong.

GB: *The selection of the Wallaby team to France contained some surprises, and caused a tirade of criticism from Queensland officials and some sections of the Queensland media. What is your reaction?*

BD: Well, it appears to me there is a hidden agenda at large in Queensland because there has been an ongoing voice of disapproval. Earlier in the year there was criticism of the Australian team's performances and lots of fingers were pointed at the coach. Then that died down—but without any apology—after we had the series win against South Africa. The same sort of comment greeted the selection of the Wallaby team to France. My reply simply is that the NSW or Queensland selectors don't pick the Australian team. I think it's a wise move to have independent selectors for the national team. They can gain benefit from the State panel as well as their own view. It's the Australian selectors' responsibility to find players who can perform at the highest level of international rugby. It's the State selectors' responsibility to find players who are capable of performing at provincial level.

GB: *Looking into your crystal ball, how does the pecking order for the 1995 World Cup shape up?*

BD: It's impossible to say at this time, but you wouldn't have to be a genius to come up with South Africa on their home turf. With what's anticipated to be their continued improvement, they're right up there. Certainly New Zealand and Australia, almost certainly France and quite probably England. I couldn't see anyone else entering into calculations with the possible exception of Western Samoa, who I know would find the hard grounds in South Africa very much to their liking—and their tackling would be very much to the *dislike* of opposition teams on those hard grounds.

* *

After figuring in the winning Bledisloe Cup side of 1949, Wallaby stalwart Cyril Burke had to wait more than four years before enjoying another Test victory.

The great day finally came at Cape Town in September 1953 when Australia downed the Springboks 18–14 to end their ten-match winning streak.

Burke had served with the RAAF in Borneo during World War II before making his Test debut against the All Blacks in 1946.

The champion Newcastle scrum-half ended his distinguished twenty-six-Test career in Brisbane against the Springboks, but playing at fly-half outside Brian Cox.

South Africa won both Tests by 9–0, scoring a pair of tries in each game.

* *

Arrivederci, Campo

One unique and remarkable rugby talent has dominated my years as a commentator. I've witnessed just about every representative match David Ian Campese has played. I've seen him at his most sublime—and doing things he'd rather forget. It's unlikely that a single player will ever help define a generation of Australian rugby in such style again.

Improvement makes straight roads, but the crooked roads without improvement are roads of genius.

William Blake, 'Proverbs of Hell'

IN 1996 David Campese became the second rugby player, after Philippe Sella, to achieve one hundred Test matches. The milestone was reached in Padua against Italy—a match won comfortably by Greg Smith's Wallabies. Campo was dropped for the subsequent Internationals against Scotland and Ireland, but regained his spot for the Wales Test after a virtuoso performance against Munster.

His last game in the old, all-gold Wallaby jumper was at

Twickenham against the Barbarians following the Welsh Test. For the second time in six days he received a standing ovation when the battle was done. Fittingly, he scored a try against the Barbarians to complete his personal rugby fairytale.

Campo is like your favourite LP record. His illustrious career has reached its twilight and although the reproduction may have become a bit crackly, the essential quality endures. On any rugby pitch he has always enjoyed being the centre of attention. As long as that athletic, fast-twitching frame can continue to react so intuitively, there will be plenty more worthwhile encores to enjoy. But . . . there does comes a time.

Beneath the public exterior of Campese lies a complex character—a loner, an extremely sensitive person, but also a supreme opportunist. His commercial successes have been well documented. After the 1991 World Cup, it was rumoured that Network Ten signed him up for three years on a six-figure annual sum, just for promotions. At the time, no rugby player past or present could claim that level of financial backing from television.

Campo is always his own man, and if you don't like the offerings then that's your problem. Criticism rarely sits well, yet he's not one to harbour grudges. Loyalty is everything. The man has learned to be a survivor and isn't shy to contact his friends in high places. How else (a cynic might ask) did he manage to take the field in the Centenary Test match against the All Blacks in Sydney, when most rugby critics placed him at no better than third or fourth in line? By all reports, coach Bob Dwyer had made it clear to his most celebrated Wallaby that 'the crooked road' had finally become a dead end. Perhaps it was divine intervention. And why not? Surely Australian Rugby owed him that modest concession. (After all, Campese's twenty-seven Tests against the All Blacks are more than any other player's in history.)

At the end of the 1987 season, the Wallabies under Alan Jones had not only 'bombed out' in the World Cup but lost a series in Argentina as well. Campese gave the ARU hierarchy a characteristic ultimatum: 'It's Jones or me. He goes, or I go.' They may be a conservative bunch at times, but the custodians of Australian rugby know their game and the value of its on-field exponents. Jones departed, Campese stayed, and Dwyer returned as coach. But, eight seasons later, Campese's relationship with the national coach deteriorated beyond repair. Privately, Campo believed the Wallabies had lost the plot. There were too many 'old men' in the forwards, he reckoned. For Dwyer's part, his star winger had simply lost the old sparkle.

By season's end all these negatives outweighed the positives and the rift was beginning to harm what had been a magnificent team spirit. Dwyer went, Campese stayed. The breakdown between these two great free spirits of rugby was a symptom of a deeper malaise that disrupted and ultimately brought down Australia's 1995 World Cup campaign.

David Campese likes to play his rugby on the highwire—without a safety net. When he slips, the result can be catastrophic. Thankfully those moments have been few, and, in overall context, insignificant. Here is a sportsman who translates rare ability into pleasure, for himself and his army of fans. The stumbles are part of the package. Campo is the embodiment of the notion that without risk there can be no adventure. When he pulls on that No. 11 rugby jumper the 'comfort zone' becomes instantly derestricted. The same applied to his close mate Mark Ella. They were both instinctive and unpredictable. My greatest regret in rugby is that those two kindred souls didn't play another five seasons or more together in Wallaby colours. Unquestionably, the firm of Campese & Ella brought together two of the greatest broken field runners of all time.

Who can forget Campese's first Test against the All Blacks at Lancaster Park, Christchurch in 1982? A cross-field kick from skipper Ella and suddenly this irreverent teenager from ACT had left the world's best winger, Stu Wilson, in his wake. Coach Dwyer had backed his judgment by choosing the youngster and in the following Test in Wellington, won 19–16 by Australia, the NZ rugby public understood why. The junior maestro handled twice in Gary Ella's try and then finished off one of the most stirring support tries in Test match history. More than half the Wallaby side handled in the movement, starting with Cox and Mark Ella. Then Gould, Grigg, Gary Ella, Hawker, Lucas, and big Steve Williams all combined before Campo scooted over beside the posts. It was a knockout blow on half-time and gave the Australians a match-winning 19–3 lead. For any remaining doubters, those tries in each of his first two Tests against the All Blacks were testimony to the arrival of an international rugby star.

But even in those formative years rough water was always close by. In the lead-up match to the third and deciding Test on that 1982 tour, the Wallabies just managed to hold out North Auckland at Whangarei by 16–12. Campese notched up two tries, a penalty and a conversion for a thirteen-point personal tally. He was duly named 'man of the match'. At the following press conference, however, coach Dwyer came out with his six-shooter blazing: 'Campese was dreadful. He used his great skills to do some brilliant things, but the rest of the match he just wasted his time. Campese was awful, absolutely bloody awful. He didn't use his head in the entire game and lost the ball in the tackle on every single occasion.'

It could only happen to Campo, and would continue to happen for the next decade or more. Because he carries everyone's highest expectations, frustration soon sets in if he falls short. There would be more of the same during the following tour of New Zealand in 1986 under Jones. After winning the first Test in Wellington, the Wallabies were robbed of a series victory in the second when Welsh referee Derek Bevan disallowed a legitimate try by Steve Tuynman. The enigmatic Jones was Campo's greatest admirer, but after a wretched day at fullback, that relationship soured. 'Today we played without a fullback,' commented Jones to a group of exhausted players in the Australian dressing room.

Later that night in Jones' room, Campo copped another withering tongue-lashing from the coach for his inept performance. So distraught was he in a nightclub a few hours later that he declared he was ready to retire from rugby. It was distressing to see such a gifted athlete and entertainer so despondent and agitated. The world's rugby enthusiasts can be grateful that Mark Ella consoled his mate that night. After switching back to wing, Campese scored the Bledisloe Cup-clinching try at Eden Park. (His replacement at fullback was Andrew Leeds, who made a smashing Test debut.)

Campo always seemed to give the impression that he was an easy target, a ready-made scapegoat for coaches when things went wrong because he was never entirely without guilt. That's the nature of his personal and sporting philosophy—sometimes dazzling, sometimes perplexing, and sometimes both in the same breath. I have always maintained that Campo's confidence must be carefully protected—'wrapped in cotton wool', if you like. When a player has the ability to perform at another level, then we have to be tolerant. That is especially true when the same individual bruises easily. Encourage rather than criticise.

But Campo's critics will be quick to parry: 'Hang on, you're talking about a gun-slinger who shoots off on a wing and a prayer. Why should we have one set of rules for Campese and another for the rest?' The point needs to be met. In a team context, Campo's star at national level certainly began to fade, especially when all his cylinders weren't firing. But it's also fair to say that at State level he's always prospered. Perhaps he feels more comfortable because among the Waratahs he's accepted for who he is and what he stands for—by team-mates, coaches and support staff who know him better. I lean towards Aristotle's theory that 'no great genius is without an admixture of madness'. The Greek philosopher also said that 'all men of genius are naturally melancholic'.

Campese is a perfectionist. He becomes frustrated when he fails to reach his self-imposed high standards on the field. He also lets himself become upset when fellow players aren't tuned in to his particular vision. But the indisputable bottom line is that he has always remained loyal to the game he loves so passionately.

My lasting memory of Campo will be his performances in the 1991 World Cup where he was named Player of the Tournament. He mesmerised the Pumas at Llanelli, humbled Wales at the Arms Park and then provided that composed 'flip ball' for Michael Lynagh in those last dramatic moments against Ireland at Lansdowne Road. His try against the All Blacks in the semi-final was pure vintage Campese. John Kirwan and his team-mates tried to second-guess Campo's intentions. He kept them guessing all the way to the goal-line. It was a mortal blow for the defending champions, a humiliation from which they never recovered. Then came that pass to Tim Horan for the try of the tournament in the same game. With the final still to play, Campo had already proved himself to be the most gifted and entertaining footballer of the era.

International rugby will never again see the likes of David Campese. Forget his faults: here is a rugby man of true distinction—a Ferrari engine in a Rolls-Royce body. My fond hope is that his flame will inspire other young players always to carry the torch to the opposition with excitement and flair. Every team needs a rebel of his ilk, someone to say, 'Let's give it a go, and bugger the consequences.'

Thanks, Campo.

Reminiscence
and Reflection

After Australia's record-breaking 26–3 win over South Africa at Newlands in 1992, Danie Craven made what would be among the last of his celebrated rugby addresses at a post-match function.

His closing words were greeted by laughter and thunderous applause. 'The Doc' was in a philosophical mood that night, but as always his reflections were laced with a typically Springbok streak of toughness.

'Many people have hoped that I will die,' he said. 'But they are mistaken. I will bury them.

'When Bernard Shaw was asked "What have you done to all the enemies you have made throughout your long life?" he replied, "I've buried the buggers!"

'So look out, you fellas. Every time I put one of you to rest, you must know the old man is *still there*.'

Not Just a Game, a Way of Life

One of the unique attractions of top-level rugby is that it is a world-wide community of friendship. That fraternity crosses all borders, but rugby is not only an international 'passport', as I first discovered in my schooldays.

BACK in early 1963, I was a second-former at Homebush Boys' High. Rugby and cricket were my great loves and I was a keen player of both.

That particular year was a significant one for Australian cricket because two NSW legends, Alan Davidson and Neil Harvey, played their last Tests. The curtain came down on those wonderful careers at the SCG in the fifth Test against England.

I couldn't resist the temptation to go out and observe this historic occasion, so on the final day of the match, a Tuesday, instead of catching the school bus I took a city-bound train. Harvey made 28 in his last Test innings. At the time his tally of Test centuries was second only to Bradman's.

After stumps were drawn I squeezed under a turnstile to gain entry to the Members' enclosure. I couldn't believe my luck. While I was standing below the window of the Australian dressing room, Wally Grout poked his head out and said, 'Hey kid, do you want these?' His two 'keeping pads' followed—a souvenir worth at least a month of schoolboy bragging.

About half an hour later 'Davo' emerged and I promptly offered to help him carry his gear to his car. As we were putting the great left-armer's bags into the boot a photographer yelled at us, 'Alan—a quick shot, please.' The flash popped, the photo taken and I thought nothing more of it.

Next day at school I was summoned to the headmaster's office. He greeted me politely and enquired about the fortunes the previous day of the school's under-fourteen cricket XI, of which I was a member. Sensing that I was in a survival situation, I explained that we'd had a good win and that I'd thoroughly enjoyed the afternoon's encounter.

Like a crafty Crown prosecutor, 'The Boss' then produced a copy of the first edition of the old Sydney *Sun* and pointed to an illustrated article on the back page. The caption read: 'Young fans farewell their hero.' There, in living black and white, was your author, resplendent in school uniform, assisting Alan Davidson load his bags into the car.

'Have a good day at the cricket, did you, Master Bray?' With sinking heart in the face of such incriminating evidence, I fell back on the last resort of all scoundrels—the truth. 'Yes I did, Sir.'

Six-of-the-best seemed unavoidable, but just at that moment the sports master, Jack Mason, stepped into the room. 'Pug' Mason (more of whom elsewhere) was coach of the first XV, which happened to be captained by my brother John. A faint flicker of hope crossed my heart. The pair of masters gave me a stern lecture before Mr Mason delivered the solemn finale.

'Johnny'—he always used to confuse me with my brother— 'if you want to play later on in my rugby team, let this be a lesson. There'll be no second chances!'

Jack was a tough, old-fashioned Australian with a wicked sense of humour. He was passionate about his rugby and very proud of his long record of success with the Homebush first XV.

One of his favourite tricks was to send a class to the gymnasium while he stayed back to lock up the change rooms. Schoolboy exuberance would soon take over and pandemonium would break out inside the gym. Our usual pastime was performing Tarzan impersonations on the climbing ropes, swinging about in all directions.

Armed with his long, thin, whippy piece of bamboo, 'Pug' would sneak into the gym and catch us red handed. The offenders—which meant most of us—then had to face the music. With sadistic glee, Mason first lined up the whole class before dealing separately with each pupil.

'Next! Bend over . . .' *WHACK!*

This ritual continued until inevitably he came to me.

'Next! Bend over . . . Johnny Bray, first XV? You're OK.'

(*You beauty!*)

'Next! Bend over . . .' *WHACK!*

Any member of the first XV was always exempt from punishment. It was an early reminder for me that rugby players, deservedly, were held in high esteem. Even at school they were already part of an exclusive brotherhood which deserved special treatment. 'Pug' Mason made sure of that.

The legendary Arthur 'Monkey' Gould managed to keep out of any serious trouble during the twenty-seven Tests he played for Wales before the turn of the century, including eighteen as captain.

But after he hung up his boots, Arthur was never far from strife.

On the occasion of his retirement, a grateful Welsh Rugby Union presented Gould with a brand new house—in recognition, they said, of his fine contribution to the game.

Well, the Irish and Scottish Rugby Unions didn't take too kindly to that gesture. They condemned it as an act of blatant professionalism, and the two home international fixtures against Wales in 1887 were cancelled.

Gould later tested his luck again when he turned his hand to refereeing.

He earned his 'Monkey' nickname while officiating in a Test between Wales and England in 1897. Somehow the crossbar became dislodged before a crucial kick at goal, so Arthur just shinnied up one post and replaced the missing spar.

Over-inflated Balls

Rugby has been a passion of mine for over thirty years. My interest in commentary started with the ABC's telecast of the club 'Match of the Day'. That redoubtable combination of Norman May and Cyril Towers was an institution in the Bray household.

I FONDLY recall Cyril Towers' preoccupation with 'over-inflated balls' at the start of each match. 'Norman,' he'd say, 'the players are having trouble with their handling because the balls are over-inflated!' And every week the officials would ignore the Gospel According to Towers and pump those balls up nice and hard again.

After each telecast I'd take my unfortunate sisters, Linda and Sarah, out into the backyard to re-enact the game with a toy rubber football which was barely inflated at all. An aggressive ten-year-old, I'd always be on the winning side and would provide a running commentary, trying to emulate Norman May's special pitch of excitement when Randwick scored a try.

We lived next door to a private hospital and the operating

theatre overlooked our backyard. I'll never forget the Saturday evening when one of 'Ken Catchpole's' kicks speared horribly off the side of my boot from the scrum-base and smashed straight through the theatre window during an operation. I'm not sure if the patient survived but it still ranks as one of my more harrowing commentating experiences.

After that incident the Matron wisely insisted we use the more spacious hospital grounds for our 'Match of the Day' replays. Who were we to argue?

Often on Sunday afternoons I'd manage to pull in a few extra players and we'd perform (always with the Bray commentary) for up to thirty patients. They'd usually flick us a few silver coins at full-time, and I hoped my strictly amateur status wasn't being compromised by these outbursts of generosity. Regrettably, the privilege of using the hospital grounds was withdrawn some years later when play went ahead one day on a very muddy pitch among rows of drying bed linen.

Muddy pitches were also something of a feature of the ABC's 'Match of the Day' telecasts of club rugby. The black-and-white images of two scrums struggling for purchase in the middle of some suburban glue-pot still linger in my mind, along with the enthusiasm of 'Nugget' May's commentary and the measured criticisms offered by Cyril Towers' successor as the 'expert', Wallaby great Trevor Allan.

Football on television in those days was a more casual business. The coverage was managed on very few cameras, and there were no video replays. If it took the production team at least a minute to flash up the new score, nobody seemed to mind. A disproportionate number of games seemed to be broadcast from Coogee Oval, perhaps because the crew only needed to cross the street for a quick beer in the Randwick Club before the long drive back to the ABC. If you were out playing or watching rugby yourself on Saturday afternoon, you could always catch up with the highlights during Allan's leisurely, ad-libbed summary during 'Sports Review' at 7.15.

And to this day, when I see an unexplained handling error in the backline, those words often come tumbling back to me through the years: 'over-inflated balls'.

- -

It was the one that got away. France's first winning international was against Scotland in Paris in 1911. But for Christian Vereilles, who'd been chosen to make his debut in that game, there would be no celebrations.

On the way to the big match he'd detected a drop-off in his energy levels and decided to buy a sandwich while the train was stopped at Lyon station. Regrettably, the train left without him and he missed the kick-off.

But there was worse news to come for the luckless Monsieur Vereille. When he finally made it to Paris he was duly informed that a second chance at playing in French colours would not be forthcoming. *Quel domage*!

- -

John Thornett's brother, Dick, represented Australia in three sports.

First, he was a member of our water polo team at the 1960 Rome Olympics. Then he served a two-year stint with the Wallabies, including a tour of South Africa and five Tests against the All Blacks.

In 1963 he turned his back on another tour of South Africa to join his younger brother Ken in rugby league with the Parramatta Eels.

Dick was occasionally troubled by stomach pains and some embarrassing complications. At one stage during the Australian tour of NZ in 1961 the problem became so acute that the Wallabies had to stop and evacuate the team bus.

On the occasion of his fortieth birthday, (and as a reminder of that fateful day), Thornett's old team-mates presented him with a canary in a cage—just in case he suffered a recurrence of the distressing ailment.

Richard is now the publican of the popular Phoenix Hotel in Woollahra, and his patrons no doubt delight in pointing an accusing finger at the canary from time to time.

High on Rugby

Every coach is forever on the lookout for that special game-plan which is guaranteed to unsettle the opposition and pave the way for victory. Even at the school level, rugby has never been short of weird and wonderful winning schemes.

ONE of the biggest thrills of my modest playing career was being selected in the school's first XV as halfback. Jack 'Pug' Mason, the first XV coach, was as good as his word. He'd promised me a firsts' spot in Year 9 after we'd won our regional premiership.

Homebush enjoyed a golden rugby era in the sixties, winning eight first-grade premierships in a row. But the real highlight was our victory in the statewide Waratah Shield in 1965. (This famous trophy had belonged to the original NSW Waratahs who toured Britain in 1927–1928.) Our arch rivals were Epping Boys' High who won a remarkable three Shields in 1967–1969. However we'd beaten them in the Zone premierships.

Jack Mason was a grizzly but inspiring character. He was nicknamed 'Pug' because of his crooked, flattened nose, the classic legacy of an outstanding football career. Sport ran in his family.

His daughter, Michelle Mason-Brown, was the Australian women's high jump champion.

One of Pug's great mates was Bryan Palmer, a former national coach who'd declined a place with the 1927–28 Waratahs because his wife was expecting their first child. Jack enlisted Palmer's assistance for our Shield campaign—and what a masterstroke it proved to be. Bryan was a colourful and charismatic type, with a lifetime of rugby knowledge to impart. But it was the instant authority of his gravel voice that set him apart. When he spoke we all listened in awe.

Bryan's approach for our final against Oak Hill College at Chatswood Oval was novel. He told the forwards he wanted them to look and feel *ugly*, starting two days before the big game. That meant not shaving or bathing.

The backs on the other hand, had to behave like show ponies, 'pretty boys' if you like. (Don't they anyway?) He didn't want to see a hair out of place (Brylcream liberally applied). Gear had to be spotless and we were to smell like flowers from after-shave lotion and deodorant when we lined up for the kick-off.

Coach Mason was now putting his faith in some new mystery energy-enhancing drink which must have been a primitive forerunner to 'Staminade'. He mixed his magic potion in the dressing room before our disbelieving eyes. Bryan, however, called an abrupt end to all this 'witch doctor' stuff when he bellowed, 'Jack, get serious! Forget that concoction stuff! My boys don't need artificial aids.'

By match time, the combination of stale body odour and perfume in our Chatswood dressing room was overwhelming, reducing one of our toughest forwards (John Symond, now managing director of Aussie Home Loans) to a state of biliousness. The forwards applied copious quantities of head tape and Vaseline and had never looked uglier. They rolled their sleeves up to their biceps and rubbed dirt on their forearms and faces, clawing at the walls and thumping each other in pent-up anger like a roomful of untamed beasts.

We backs—the show ponies—discreetly kept out of their way. I'd boiled my white shorts and boot tape in a saucepan of bleach-and-water the night before so that they were absolutely snow-white. We were high on fragrance and all that remained was a last-minute check of hair.

Twenty minutes before kick-off we lined up in front of the mirror Indian file. I waited, and waited . . . and waited. After five minutes my five-eighth became extremely agitated. 'What's the hold up?' I asked. 'It's the bloody referee. He's taking half an hour to comb his hair!' Sure enough, there was the ref, poised before the mirror, ensuring that every last hair was in place. His identity? None other than Dr Roger Vanderfield, the great Test referee and past chairman of the International Rugby Board. Roger was always immaculately groomed and when he had finally completed his meticulous coiffure we trailed out after him onto the field.

I don't actually remember much about the game itself except that we won 6–3. Oak Hill had succumbed to the stench of our forwards and were 'seduced' by the overpowering perfume of the backs. If ever a match was won before the kick-off then this was it. To a man we were all convinced that Bryan's 'magic' formula could not fail.

Perhaps it was a 'one-off' masterplan, but in hindsight it may be worth resurrecting. Then again, how the All Black and Springbok packs might react to clouds of after-shave is debatable. We wouldn't want to do anything to niggle them, now would we?

The 1921 Springboks were the first South African national team to visit Australia, but they didn't get to play against the Wallabies.

They were en route to New Zealand and their itinerary included three successive matches against the NSW Waratahs. Each of those fixtures resulted in a convincing victory for the visitors.

Their skipper back then was another classy Pienaar—Theo—who despite the protests of his team-mates stood himself down from the Tests across the Tasman because he felt he was not a good enough player!

The 1937 Springboks rank with the greatest touring sides of all time.

Their gruelling twenty-six-match tour of Australia and New Zealand yielded just two losses and historic victories in the Test series on both sides of the Tasman.

Their only loss in Australia was to NSW on a heavy SCG surface, in driving rain. The Waratahs were able to overcome the conditions to play a slick handling game in the backs.

The great NSW centre Cyril Towers turned in a superb game to orchestrate four tries by the Waratah wingers.

But that brilliant 1937 Springboks team didn't take long to bounce back.

In New Zealand they won twelve matches on the trot, the climax being a series-clinching 17–6 win in the third Test at Eden Park. A record crowd of 58,000 watched that stirring clash.

Rugby *Realpolitik*

A quarter of a century ago the Australian sporting world was very different. The pace was more measured, traditions still counted and the ABC was the undisputed leader in sports broadcasting. For me, joining that elite team was a dream come true.

ON MY first day on the job with ABC Sport back in 1969 I walked into the city office and there, before my eyes, were three legendary commentators: Alan McGilvray, doyen of cricket broadcasters; Geoff Mahoney, the velvet voice of racing; and the one and only Norman May. There was enough reflected glory from those great stars for me to feel I was already basking in limelight.

In truth, the first twelve months were rather dull—mainly observation and endless hours of recording 'practice tapes'. But the social and sporting side of the job was excellent. Among many pleasures, I'd discovered that the ABC had an annual rugby clash with Federal Parliament.

Until I joined the ABC I'd been playing with Eastern Suburbs club in Sydney, but I had to give up grade football because of my new career. Nevertheless, my appetite for a game of rugby was undiminished so I presented my credentials to the organisers of the Parliament match, who promptly named me as the ABC's halfback.

We travelled to Canberra by bus, confident we had the side to retain the prestigious trophy. Unfortunately though, some malicious stirrer had started a rumour that Ken Catchpole would be playing as a 'guest' on our side. We arrived at the venue and manager Bob 'Rocket' Moore, the well-known radio announcer, stepped off the bus—and immediately shot back on board, in a state of shock.

'Wrong ground! There's four thousand bloody people out there!' It was the right ground, but the wrong scrum-half.

Not to be outdone, however, the parliamentarians had stacked their side with 'ring-ins', most of whom were Aussie Rules players. All we seemed to do throughout the afternoon was turn around and retrieve seventy-metre kicks. The effort told and we eventually lost 36–3.

The highlight of the game was an early altercation in the front row. The front three for Federal Parliament comprised Ian Sinclair (later leader of the Country Party), Bill Hayden (the later Governor General) as hooker, and Doug Anthony (later Deputy Prime Minister). Tempers inevitably frayed in the scrums and our loosehead prop, one Bill McGowan, finally did his block and thumped Hayden.

'You can't do that, mate,' exclaimed our tighthead. 'He's a politician.'

'I couldn't give a stuff who he is!'

Bill Hayden—ex-Queensland policeman, future Treasurer, Leader of the Opposition and Vice-Regal Personage—demonstrated the admirable restraint of the born politician and refrained from retaliation. How different Australian political history might have been had Hayden got stuck in and the fisticuffs made their way into the media!

Not surprisingly the ABC v Parliament fixture was allowed to lapse for some years while tempers cooled. When hostilities were resumed in 1981 I recall we exacted satisfactory revenge, perhaps through the efforts of a few very 'short-term' ABC employees— namely Wallabies Bill Calcraft, Ross Reynolds, Phillip Cox and James Black.

Always on the look out for a sure thing, Geoff Mahoney had quietly secured odds of 2–1 on an ABC victory. We didn't let him down, winning 54–0. I played five-eighth outside Cox and also won a useful little side bet with my inside centre. I'd wagered that I wouldn't be tackled—or actually have to tackle someone else—during the entire game.

Perhaps our opponents had kept in mind that most persuasive of all political maxims: 'Discretion is the better part of valour.'

● ●

The Fiji rugby squad departed for the 1987 World Cup amid great political turmoil in their own country. For many of the players this was their first trip abroad. Team members all had to observe a strict curfew which didn't even allow for telephone calls back home.

But despite these restrictions, the Fijians won their opening match against Argentina 28–9. The total population of the Fiji islands was just one million, while Argentina had drawn its rugby side from close to twenty-six million.

Regrettably, that David-and-Goliath glory was short-lived. The Fijians lost their next match to New Zealand 74–13.

■ ■

··

For those who've been on the wrong end of a real rugby shellacking, some statistics to cheer you up from the 1995 World Cup.

Tuesday 11 October 1994 remains the blackest day in the history of Singapore rugby. They lost their World Cup qualifier in Kuala Lumpur against Hong Kong by 164–13. It was the highest Test score in history. The total—177 points—was also the largest ever. Hong Kong's fullback, Ashley Billington, scored ten tries—the most by an individual in any Test match.

Japan became the sixteenth and last team to make the 1995 World Cup by winning the Malaysian tournament. They were later to lose to the All Blacks at Bloemfontein by 145–17 (twenty-one tries to two). Simon Culhane kicked a world record twenty conversions on debut. Marc Ellis scored six tries and the half-time score was 84–3.

······································

24-Carat Nugget

One of the most endearing qualities of the old ABC was that it tolerated reasonable amounts of larrikinism, eccentricity and even excess. Good broadcasting demands strong personalities, and the best sports broadcasters were invariably genuine 'characters'. Among them, one always stood out...

HE'S NOT only been one of Australia's most colourful commentators, but also been one of the very best. Norman 'Nugget' May's great qualities are an encyclopaedic memory for sporting facts and figures, natural enthusiasm and unique communication skills behind a microphone.

My first experience with Norman in the commentary box was as a scorer on the ABC's Rugby Match of the Day at Manly Oval in the early seventies. The telecast was scheduled to start at 2.55 p.m. but with just five minutes remaining, there was still no sign of Nugget or his expert commentator, Ken Catchpole. The director in the ABC outside broadcast van was an unflappable English–born gentleman named Bill Phillips. In between gentle puffs on his ever-present pipe I heard his cultured voice come through my earphones. 'Gordon, dear boy, you'll have to call this game if 'Nugget' doesn't front.' The instant, eager reply: 'No worries Bill, I'd love to.'

But just at that moment I heard a screech of tyres behind the scaffolding which supported the commentary position. I poked my head over the back and sure enough there was the Norman May Ferrari, as he called it (actually a battered, faded red Datsun). The vehicle was also instantly recognisable because much of Norman's wardrobe was on the back seat—jumpers, coats, ties and even a pair of slippers!

With less than two minutes to go before 'on-air' he climbed the ladder, hotly pursued by 'Catchy'. Casually he pulled on his headphones, adjusted the mike and flicked the appropriate switches. After a short pause he spoke to the director. 'May here. Standing by.' The reply, 'Roll opening titles . . . ready Norman . . . take your own cue.' The show was on the road with no apparent ripple. 'Welcome to Manly Oval where the famous seaside club take on Northern Suburbs. And I must say we've just witnessed one of the best reserve grade games of the year with Manly winning by a point, 16–15.'

I nearly fell off the chair. After the game I turned to my boyhood idol and said, 'Norman, I'm pretty disappointed. How could you make that comment when you didn't even see the reserve grade match?' His reply: 'Yes I did! We were watching from the RSL club across the road!'

It was vintage 'Nugget'. (And for those still wondering, the reason Norman finally left his beloved ABC was that his modest public service salary could no longer support his taste for vintage champagne. Absolutely true.)

The Sweet Smell of Success

Thirty or so years ago the camaraderie and amateur traditions of grade rugby in Sydney meant that anyone playing the game was likely to share a dressing room with some incredible characters. For a keen young halfback, the eighty minutes out in the middle were often the simple bit.

IN 1968, after leaving high school, my rugby fortunes led me to Woollahra Oval, home of the 'Easts Beasties'. Celebrated Wallaby Peter 'Charlie' Crittle was still playing, and very successfully at that. The following year he led the Tri-colours to premiership honours and was a regrettable omission from the ill-fated tour of South Africa. Easts' loyal fans have been waiting patiently ever since for another championship triumph.

Puckish barrister Barney Walsh was our first-grade coach. He and his wife lived in a flat on the corner of Forbes and William Streets in Darlinghurst. This of course meant that he was ideally situated to join the commentary staff of the ABC Sports Department for regular weekly refreshment just down the road at the famous Gladstone Hotel. The 'Glad' is no more, but back then it was the unofficial headquarters of ABC Radio—actors, producers, journalists and broadcasters all mixed in the beery atmosphere of a classic, rough-and-ready inner-Sydney pub.

Barney's affection for Easts was contagious. He was an inspiration for an ambitious young player like myself. The hard-baked turf off O'Sullivan Road in Rose Bay became my rugby shrine—a place to realise my dreams. Even, one day, to appear on the ABC's 'Match of the Day' as Easts' first grade halfback. After languishing in the fifths for several weeks, the selectors—I'm sure with a bit of encouragement from Barney—found a place for me at scrum-half in the fourth-grade XV, rubbing shoulders for the first time with the legendary Michael 'Bread' Rowles.

Mick's career was well established and as he was playing in the second row at that stage we hardly had a lot in common. He was also every halfback's nightmare—a lock whose attachment to gravity was such that he could never quite bring himself to jump in the lineout. Coach Mal Stenning, a first-grade opening bowler with Waverley during the off-season, always delivered a forceful pre-match address before 'Bread' stepped in with his final gee-up as skipper. I vividly recall the sight of our captain, false teeth discarded, gumming us about how we had to believe in ourselves and get stuck into the opposition. Nevertheless, 'Bread' had a real charm about him, although to be perfectly honest I think it was more to do with his off-field dedication to personal hygiene than any late-blooming rugby ability manifesting itself in fourth grade.

For those who haven't met the affable Mick Rowles, picture a fair-skinned, wide-bodied ex-tight-forward with an old neck ailment—a stiffness which limits his neck rotation. The affliction is no doubt a legacy of those hundreds of occasions when he turned around after a ruck only to see all that good work from the forwards spoilt by over-ambitious backs. 'Bread' is a big man. His weight has increased since his playing days.

He's a much-loved character in Eastern Suburbs territory, and is now one of Sydney's most successful real estate agents with the Bradfield and Prichard firm of Double Bay. Michael was elected president of Easts in 1988 and his continuing influence in the tough world of sports club management is a tribute to his leadership and example. But it was as a player in the late sixties and seventies that Mick Rowles really captured my imagination.

'Bread's' pre-game ritual had me spellbound. He'd begin by carefully unpacking his neatly-pressed shorts, like a father cradling his new-born baby for the first time, followed by his shiny boots with a new set of snow-white laces. Here was a man who took great pride in his personal appearance.

Each step of his match preparation was carried out with precision and unchanging regularity. After he'd hoisted his socks into position, fixed below his knees by a pair of tight rubber gerters, the team manager would throw him his coveted No. 4 jumper. It was as if he'd just accepted the crown jewels—or a match-winning pass. And when Mick finally moved to the mirror in the toilet area, you knew you had exactly four minutes to evacuate the dressing room.

Let me explain. After he'd carefully rubbed Vaseline into every exposed piece of his freckled pink flesh, 'Bread' would apply a white halo of masking tape around his forehead and his grizzly ears (which had definitely packed into a few scrums too many). Mick was always last out of the dressing room, and with good reason. His grooming routine in front of the mirror before the warm-up climaxed with a fearful venting of internal gases. The rest of us were long gone by then but the remnants from that thunderous procedure still lingered when the team returned to the dressing room twenty minutes later.

Fortunately Mick's dressing room demeanour became more environmentally friendly after the game. The eight showers in Easts' home dressing room were communal. As you'd expect from a forward with something of a fetish for personal cleanliness,

'Bread' always monopolised the lone cake of soap and his stint under the shower often lasted longer than that of some of the more fastidious backs who formed the second shift.

Rugby players behave differently when they strip off in a dressing room, especially after the game. Some modestly leave their towels tucked around their hips as they step into their underpants, while others prefer to face the wall. Only a small percentage have no inhibitions. 'Bread' was unashamedly one of the last category. Obviously proud of his well-nourished torso, he'd spend up to ten minutes or so in a state of total undress after his shower, working his towel from head to toe in a vigorous display of drying power. Then the real fun and games began.

First, Mick's special tinea powder was applied in liberal doses. If you weren't in the club enjoying your first beer by this point then your whole evening could be tainted by his robust application of this and the Johnson's Baby Powder that followed. Clouds of the stuff engulfed the dressing room. Then came skin moisturiser, deodorant and aftershave lotion, and another session in front of the mirror for the finishing touches—a correct part in his gleaming shampooed hair, a meticulous cleaning of his teeth and a mouth gargle with Listerine to round off.

When 'Bread' finally walked into the club, it was like the Second Coming—he simply oozed health, complemented by an overpowering aroma of perfumes and baby powder. In those days I didn't consider luxuries like deodorant on my ABC trainee's salary of $29 per week, so you can imagine how guilty I felt when Mick moved majestically alongside me at the bar to order his first beer. And late into the night, even on his tenth schooner, 'Bread' would still be smelling like a rose—a great club man demonstrating all the qualities of a future president.

(By the way, if you're curious about my attention to observational detail in the dressing room, put it down to a future commentator's peripheral vision. For the record, I preferred to get my undies on as quickly as possible!)

Soon after, my grade rugby days were rather swiftly curtailed by the Head of ABC Sport, the late Bernard Kerr. 'Choose between playing and a broadcasting career, son!' he snapped one Monday morning. My time with Easts was over, but happily those gruff words did not spell the end of my playing association with Michael Rowles.

The ABC fielded a team in the now-defunct Journalists' Cup competition. Opposition teams included the *Sun-Herald*, captained by well known journalist and publisher Gary Lester, the *Telegraph*, *Daily Mirror* and Channel Nine. As you'd expect, the friendly rivalry sometimes got out of hand. We played rugby league, but under union ethics. The idea was that we had to behave like gentlemen. I wish someone had explained that idea to Nine's music maestro, Geoff Harvey.

Our local derby with the Channel Nine boys was willing enough, but always clean and hard. That is, until late in the game when I was tackled head-on by Mr Harvey. Included in the package was a stinging and none-too-subtle uppercut to my chin. His South African origins had surfaced. Suddenly, my unblemished record of on-field discipline was in the balance.

My immediate reaction was, 'You bastard, Harvey!' I'm not proud to admit it now, but I'd snapped. As I rose with the ball tucked under my right arm I unleashed a fierce left rip into his solar plexus. He buckled over with an a loud and distinctly unmusical screech.

Regrettably this unsavoury incident occurred right under the nose of the worldly first-grade referee, Laurie Bruyeres. After delivering a sharp rebuke, he pointed his finger in the direction of the dressing room. 'But sir, he started it,' I pleaded desperately, but both of us marched off for an early shower. I don't condone what I did, however to this day I also don't regret it. There comes a time when you can only take so much. (And besides, the villain definitely came off second-best.)

But back to 'Bread' Rowles. On the morning of our big clash with the *Telegraph* (captained by the impressive second rower Ian Heads), two of our forwards pulled out. A few hasty phone calls led to the last-minute arrival of our hero for what he claimed was to be his first-ever game of rugby league. Unfortunately there was no mirror in the dressing shed, so Mick was forced to take the field without his usual preparation.

'Bread' took the ball up all day. He had a blinder and couldn't believe how much fun it was to actually run with the ball. Mick played three more games with us and none of our opponents ever challenged his bona fides as an ABC staff member. We told them he was a night cleaner at the Commission's old William St premises. Journalists will believe *anything*.

But the honour of contributing the best-ever performance on a Journalists' Cup day belongs to the smooth-talking ex-ABC broadcaster Bob 'Rocket' Moore. He'd left home at 9.15 a.m. to pick up some bread for the family breakfast. En route he noticed some familiar faces when driving past the local footy oval. With all good intentions he pulled over and dropped in—and was still there eight hours later—without the bread, but thoughtfully tending the last keg with all his customary skill and flair. Time does tend to slip by—especially when you're having fun.

A Lucky Break

After I completed my two-year cadetship as a specialist trainee with ABC Sport in Sydney, the Commission promptly dispatched me in its wisdom to Hobart. I enjoyed my years in the Apple Isle, but might have languished there forever had it not been for a particularly timely accident.

FRESH off the plane in Hobart, one of my first priorities was to establish contact with a local rugby club. This turned out to be the mighty Associates—a fine body of dedicated rugby men including a sprinkling of refugee 'mainlanders'.

I rolled up at training and briefly outlined my playing background as a recent third-grade halfback with Eastern Suburbs. The local officials immediately offered me a trial with the State squad, which I declined on the grounds that I was already scheduled to commentate on Tasmania's forthcoming matches in the Southern States carnival!

There were eight first-grade teams in the Hobart competition at the time and the rugby community was understandably close-knit. There were no clubhouses, just a friendly pub where 'mine host' produced little extras like complimentary hot finger food after training and on match days. These were, of course, a mere prelude to the far more serious business of consuming heroic quantities of Cascade beer. Tasmanian rugby players can hold their own with the best when it comes to 'boat races'.

It didn't take long to realise that Tasmania was Aussie Rules mad. My new ABC boss, the legendary local commentator Don Closs, said I would have to forget about rugby and start concentrating on the 'real' game with an eye to becoming a regular describer. I like to think I took this blow manfully and launched myself into the unique atmosphere of Australian Rules football with zeal. It was a formidable challenge for a young man steeped in rugby.

So rugby was cast aside (apart from the odd coaching session at city high schools), as I dutifully attended training sessions of the Tasmanian Football League clubs. I talked to players and even pulled on my rugby boots on several occasions to join the Aussie Rules stars. Within a few months of arriving in Hobart (and after attending a seminar on laws of the game—yes, there are some) the stage was finally set for my debut behind the microphone as a TFL commentator.

The venue for the occasion was Boyer Oval, New Norfolk, about twenty kilometres out of Hobart, where the locals were taking on North Hobart. Although extremely nervous, I was primed for an inspired first-up performance. After he'd called the first ten minutes or so my enthusiastic boss, Mr Closs, handed over. 'And now, to continue the description here at Boyer, here's our new rugby commentator from Sydney—Gordon Bray!' My slim credibility had been utterly destroyed by those few unfortunate words.

My head started spinning. After building up my adrenalin to the necessary pitch, I suddenly felt like a stunned mullet. I still can't recall feeling so deflated during a commentary. Try as I did over the next few seasons, I'm not sure I ever achieved full credibility with the local footie fans. I even played a few social games but seemed to spend an inordinate amount of time running around for very little contact with the ball. Yet my colleague Drew Morphett succeeded where I failed. He was educated at the exclusive Scots' College in Sydney where he displayed real talent as scrum-half for the first XV. But unlike me he took to Aussie Rules like a duck to water and is still one of our most accomplished AFL commentators.

However, all was not lost for this passionate supporter of the fifteen-man game. The year following my arrival in Tasmania presented a cherished opportunity to show off my submerged rugby heritage. The touring French team was visiting Hobart and the ABC Sports Department had decided to present a live telecast of the game. The 'expert' commentator was my local dentist, a chap named George Debenham. He also happened to be the President of the Tasmanian Rugby Union and a former player with Associate's fierce rivals, Taroona. Fortunately our rivalry didn't spill over into the commentary box (which was an open-air vantage point perched atop a fifteen-metre-high scaffold at Bellerive Oval—now Hobart's international cricket ground).

The local side was dwarfed by the French XV, whose second row contained the celebrated—and gigantic—Spanghero brothers, Walter and Claude. Our Tasmanian rugby community turned out in force (around three thousand), but no-one was prepared for the dramatic opening to the game. After just three minutes winger Ian 'Snakes' Hawkes charged down a kick and scored in the corner.

The crowd went berserk and so did the commentators. George's false teeth fell out, which was hardly a good advertisement for local dentistry. In the excitement the legs of my chair slipped between the temporary floorboards of the commentary position, pitching me precariously close to the edge of our broadcast 'tower'. As I clung to the chair it was almost as if I'd scored the try myself. 'What a wonderful moment for Tasmanian rugby!' I shrieked. But the Apple Isle's elation was to be short-lived. France then proceeded to dominate the match, emerging victorious by a handsome forty-point margin.

My stay in Tasmania lasted four years and eventually provided the lucky break everyone needs to launch their broadcasting career. It came in 1974 when the ABC decided it was time to blood one of their young commentators in its coverage of the Commonwealth Games in Christchurch. To my great dismay that honour went to a Hobart colleague, Graham McNaney, who subsequently carved out a very successful entrepreneurial career with the crack Melbourne Magic basketball team.

'Macca' decided to hold a celebration party before his departure for New Zealand. Things went swimmingly until he was cooking my steak and a loose brick fell off the barbecue straight onto his big toe. Fortunately for me—though not for him—he was only wearing thongs so a break was inevitable. Next day he was ruled unfit to travel and I was selected as his last-minute replacement in the ABC team.

Who knows where I might have ended up if I'd declined Graham's kind invitation to attend his farewell that day. Perhaps as an AFL commentator in Melbourne with Channel Seven? I don't think so—the call of rugby is just too strong. But the Apple Isle will always be etched in my fondest broadcasting memories, not the least for the genuinely lucky break it provided.

Escape to King Island

The worldwide community of rugby has outposts in the strangest places. One of the most enjoyable aspects of my job is that over the years I've been lucky enough to visit many of them. Invariably, the more obscure and out-of-the-way my rugby destination, the better the fun.

HAVING become very attached to Tasmania after my four-year stint there, I try to visit my 'home away from home' whenever possible. Often it's as a guest speaker or in a rugby fund-raising capacity. My friends and acquaintances in the Apple Isle are very important to me because they epitomise the true spirit of rugby football. They may be a national backwater of the sport, but boy, do they know how to enjoy themselves on and off the paddock!

In 1988 I was invited by Associates Club in Hobart to referee their forthcoming fixture against their rivals on King Island, a rugged and forbidding piece of landscape in Bass Strait. At stake was the King Island Cup—not quite the Bledisloe but important nevertheless—and 'would the ABC be interested in covering the momentous event?'

Any excuse for a rugby trip. The then Head of ABC TV Sport, David Salter, said yes but queried: 'How do you propose to call a rugby Test between Australia and New Zealand at Concord Oval and then cover a match on King Island next day?'

'Not a problem,' quoth Bray.

In truth, the transport logistics presented major problems. The ABC's helicopter pilot, Gary Ticehurst, had to negotiate special permission to land on the Test pitch at Concord twenty minutes after full-time. This allowed me just enough time to record my 'links' on-site for the TV replay next day. (In truth, I was pleased to be out of the Concord cauldron that afternoon because 'Buck' Shelford's All Blacks had walloped the Australians 31–9 to wrap up the series.)

The evacuation went smoothly. After an eight-minute chopper flight yours truly and producer Colin Rodgers landed on the tarmac at Mascot and were driven straight to our aircraft for a 5.45 p.m. departure to Hobart via Devonport. Not your average 'day in the life of a sports commentator', but the promise of reffing a rugby match in the middle of Bass Strait was just too tantalising to miss.

The following morning we teamed up with the Associates players and flew in two light aircraft to King Island. The match was played on a windswept cow paddock in chilly conditions. The goal posts comprised rough-hewn paperbark saplings finely balanced forward into the teeth of a 'Roaring Forties' gale. Club members roamed the field before kick-off removing scores of cowpats. The opposition included several expatriate Maoris who all, predictably, claimed to have been All Black trialists.

Meanwhile, the ABC fitted me up with a microphone so I could record a commentary 'on-the-run' for the television coverage. Wags in the crowd suggested this was possibly a 'World First'. It also offered the unique opportunity for the commentator to disagree with his own rulings as referee—a classic conflict of interests if ever I've seen one!

The contest had some bright flowing moments (when the backs actually saw the ball), but foremost it was a battle 'up front'. Big Brother from the Tasmanian mainland was intent on putting the island minnows in their place. At one stage, play remained rooted to the same spot for at least ten minutes while the forwards got to know each other. This must have been riveting stuff for the curious locals who'd encircled the ground in their cars.

'Sokes' (the Associates) eventually won the King Island Cup after a willing but good-spirited contest—and despite conceding a penalty try when their captain, Michael Keating, tripped the referee. The telecast was duly aired nationally the following week in our regular program, *Sunday Rugby*, and generated much favourable comment amongst the rugby community.

Five weeks later I was delighted to receive the Sydney Referees' Association's Annual Gold Deviate Award. This coveted prize is confined to members of that august body. The citation read: 'For Blatant Self-Promotion on National TV Whilst Masquerading as a Member of the SRA. Awarded to Gordon Bray.'

Not quite the Order of Australia, but nonetheless hard-earned.

In his classic memoirs Viewless Winds, 1908 Wallaby tour captain Herb Moran was generous in victory after Australia's three-tries-to-one victory at Blackheath. With a clever rhetorical twist, he approached the moment from his opponent's perspective:

'No-one can deny that an Englishman wins splendidly and I am not sure that this is not the harder test. He accepts success as his due, is never cock-a-hoop, never triumphs clamorously. With perfect manners he commends the loser's great display; was it not quite worth of the example he, himself, had set the world? But you will not conceive many sporting people outside England that in their severely precise measurement of sporting conduct the Englishman does not use a special pair of callipers for those who come from outside.'

Memorabilia Madness

Did you know that beach rugby is an official sport in Portugal? Or that rugby matches are regularly played on the floor of the Dead Sea, 385 metres below sea level? People who devote much of their spare time to collecting arcane information like that are decidedly odd. As for those who happily spend thousands of dollars on collecting rugby memorabilia, well, what can I say?

RUGBY has been around in various forms for over a thousand years. In AD 881 Emperor Hsi Tsung sentenced an officer to death for the crime of describing an early version of football as 'unseemly'. In Central and South America, the Mayan and Aztec cultures were playing a football game with a rubber ball one thousand years before rugby as we know it developed in Great Britain. In North America, the Indians were engaging in their own brand of football as early as the seventeenth century, with up to a thousand players divided into two teams, fighting over a small deerskin ball.

As an international sport rugby knows no boundaries. The code is played in an estimated 120 countries and the scope for memorabilia is endless. It provides opportunities for collectors of all ages, no matter what your budget. For example, you can obtain Five Nations programs for as little as $4, or at the other end of the scale, an acquaintance of mine will sell you a large portrait photograph of the 1924 'Invincibles' All Blacks, in original condition and surrounded by the personal autographs of the team. Yours for just $2,000.

A fellow collector in New Zealand, Geoff Miller, regularly receives lengthy telephone calls from a certain 'Walter' in Italy. He apparently works for that country's Telstra equivalent and his privileged position allows him to cast his worldwide net unhindered. Walter's particular passion is for collecting rugby lapel badges. 'He's probably got several thousand now from all over the world,' Geoff told me. 'I've sent him a number of New Zealand badges and in return, without me asking, he's forwarded the badges of some of the more obscure rugby-playing countries—Andorra, Tunisia, Poland, Denmark and Morocco.

'He also sent me historical publications including the histories of rugby in Czechoslovakia and the former Yugoslavia. But my personal favourite is *Fifty Years of Rugby History in Italy*. When the book arrived (written in Italian of course), I opened it up to a chapter entitled "La Fantasic All Blacks". On the opposite page was a lovely photograph of former NZ halfback Kevin Green. Kevin lives around the corner from me in Hamilton. In the same publication I came across some Test matches played between Italy, Germany and Romania in 1940. A few years later the matches were repeated and the referee for Italy and Romania was appointed by the Führer.'

Like myself, Geoff has something of a fetish for discovering trivia. When researching for the 1991 Rugby World Cup, I came across some absolute gems in the American Eagles handbook. They proved invaluable for my commentary during the dramatic International in Dublin between Australia and Ireland. When fellow commentator Chris Handy said, 'No matter where you're watching, on the North Pole or the South Pole ...', I was able to chip in with '... and talking of Poles, did you know that Pope John Paul played international rugby for Poland?'

Collecting rugby memorabilia and trivia has many facets, and many surprises as well. For instance, did you know that the Webb Ellis Cup does not have a long and illustrious rugby history, but is, in fact, a larger replica of an old trophy found in a London antique store which was purchased for the purpose of becoming the model for the World Cup? The individual after whom it was named, Reverend William Webb Ellis, is recognised in the annals of rugby union as being the first person to run with the ball in his hands. By this act alone in 1823 at Rugby School, from which the code took its name, he created the distinctive feature of the game as we know it today. Although not a great deal is known of Ellis's life, he seems to have been a bit of an unreliable rule-breaker, as indicated in a letter which hinted of his shifty behaviour in school exams. He died in relative obscurity in France in 1872.

The ball with which Webb ran was a soccer ball, since the use of an oval ball did not enter the official laws of rugby until 1893. Prior to this there has been some confusion, causing the editor of *Bell's Life* in London to reprimand a publisher for being unaware that 'rugby is played with an oval ball'.

There was no such confusion, however, when the Maori rugby team travelled to Great Britain in 1888. They wore feathered cloaks and chanted their war cry, all of which was considered to be in rather bad taste by the Poms who criticised such behaviour as 'the circus element which isn't needed'. The *Illustrated Sporting and Dramatic News* carried a report of the New Zealanders' first match against Surrey on October 3, 1888, which read in part:

The mainly English game of football is practised with spirit in New Zealand not only by the colonists and their sons of our own race but some of the new civilised generation of Maoris. In the New Zealand team of football players there is a mixture of the two races, colonial and native. They are dressed in black knickerbockers and jerseys, which in the case of the Maoris gives them a rather sombre aspect; but they are men of fine growth, well-knit and well proportioned, and are skilled adepts in all points of the game.

All sounds pretty familiar, doesn't it?

Former Wallaby International and fellow rugby memorabilia nut Peter Crittle has one of the finest rugby book collections in the world. Since 1960 he's also been gathering a selection of programs and estimates he has about 70 per cent of Australia's Test match programs since the turn of the century.

'I enjoy the hunt like any collector, and the prize that goes with the outcome,' he said. The fifty-seven-year-old barrister has always had a fascination for history, having majored in the subject at Sydney University. 'I go to enormous lengths to track down books. There have been many trips overseas for book auctions. I'm off to Christchurch this weekend to try to pick up a couple of items.'

Like any collector, Crittle has developed a vast range of contacts around the globe. 'One of the most exciting times for me is receiving the monthly catalogues. I have subscriptions in a large number of places including New Zealand, Britain and France. I recall Mr Keating [the former Australian Prime Minister] saying the same thing about catalogues and his love of French Empire clocks.'

Well-known sporting collector and dealer Tony Burgess, from the Sydney Antique Centre, is another who has a particular passion for rugby. 'I judge the enjoyment of a holiday by the amount of things I pick up,' he told me. His favourite expedition moment occurred in Cairo. 'I was browsing through an old wares shop when I came across a rugby spelter [a small sculpture cast in zinc alloy]. He was the epitome of a back rower or centre, running like the wind, with the ball under one arm. I picked him up for the equivalent of $250.'

Other outstanding pieces acquired by Tony during his travels have been a 1921 Manly rugby union district cap, and a photograph of the 1963 Wallaby team to South Africa personally signed by players and officials. 'That side was special as I grew up in that era. The team's performance in drawing the series two-all was quite magnificent,' he said. (By happy coincidence, Peter Crittle was a distinguished member of that famous campaign.) Burgess also has some words of advice for autograph collectors. 'If you want David Campese to sign a program after the match, remember to get him to date it as well. It's a far more significant collector's piece because he's done it on the day.'

Having collected rugby memorabilia for over twenty years, though only seriously for the last ten, I can confirm the splendid excitement of the hunt and then the capture. After establishing a network of contacts in New Zealand, I was delighted to receive a trunk call one morning from across the Tasman just before 6 a.m. My wife did not, perhaps, share my pre-dawn glee. The caller told me he'd been browsing through an antique store in Auckland and had come across a plaster figurine of a French rugby player from the 1924 Olympics. The paintwork was a little chipped but the little figure had a lot of character. Knowing of my hobby, he'd taken the trouble to find my telephone number through Radio New Zealand. He also offered to purchase it for me. (The asking price was NZ$500. We eventually got it for $450.)

I can't describe my joy when I first set eyes on him. We've christened him Jean-Pierre, after the great French captain Jean-Pierre Rives. His face conveys the same pride and determination. With the hindsight of history, I'd suggest he must have been made before the 1924 final. In front of 40,000 fans at Colombes Stadium in Paris on 18 May 1924, the United States shocked the French with a 17–3 victory, scoring five tries to one. The crowd was so upset that they booed during the US national anthem. One of the American players couldn't receive his gold medal because he was knocked out by a blow from a disgruntled Frenchwoman's umbrella. On second thoughts, perhaps Jean-Pierre's pose depicts his reaction during that anthem!

Programs are probably the most popular objects of rugby memorabilia collecting. Geoff Miller once had a startling request from a collector in Wales. He recalls: 'A few years ago, just before Wales toured New Zealand, I offered to pick up a couple of programs for this chap from each of the tour games. He wrote back asking for twenty of the provincial games and fifty of the Test matches. The cost came out to NZ$500. I sent a letter back requesting an advance, and thought at the time: that's the last I'll hear of the matter.

'Three days before the first tour match, a padded brown parcel arrived, completely unregistered. I opened it and out spilt NZ$500 in crisp new notes. Our association has developed since then. When Scotland toured New Zealand two years later I collected about $2,500 worth of programs for him. He now runs a successful mail order business selling them at three times their face value.'

There is no commercial imperative behind my memorabilia collection. In fact, I've found that swapping material with collectors is more enjoyable than buying because you tend to get better value all round. Of course, acquisition-through-exchange is not always possible and as a rugby enthusiast I'm always on the look out for something different. Jerseys, old photos, books, stamps, posters, trophies—*anything* rugby. Perhaps when I'm too old and croaky to get behind a microphone any more I might consider arranging my collection into a museum-type display. In the meantime I'll continue my hunt for another Jean-Pierre.

A Wallaby at Last!

To those who might think that travelling the world commentating and reporting on rugby must be a marvellous occupation, you're dead right. And just when you think you've savoured all the glories of the international game, yet another mouth-watering invitation comes along...

AN ALL-EXPENSES paid trip to Bermuda with the Classic Wallabies—'and bring your boots in case we need you'—was an enticing scenario. The organisers of the World Rugby Classic had agreed to subsidise myself and an ABC cameraman in return for a television documentary of the 1990 tournament. Absolutely impossible to resist.

Eligible players had to be over thirty-four years old and have reached International status. There were no problems raising the numbers 'Down Under'. The twenty-six-strong squad was captained by Mark Loane and bristled with exceptional talent from bygone eras. In the forwards, men such as 'Topo' Rodriguez, David Hillhouse and Duncan Hall, while the backline featured the legendary names of Russell Fairfax, Paul McLean and Kenny Wright.

Our stopover in Los Angeles included a visit to an L.A. Rams training session arranged by our number-one halfback, Peter Carson. 'Carso' was then the current coach of the NSW backline and he presumably thought the gridiron experts might have something to teach us. The Rams workout was conducted with military precision, with every movement videoed by cameras in high towers. Security paranoia meant we weren't allowed to film any activity other than the 'warm-down' and general scenes in the dressing room.

Some of the big African-American players looked like over-sized Tarzans. Former Randwick back John Berne, a delightful first-generation Irishman who later played league with Souths and Easts, enquired at one point, 'Did you get a close look at that big black guy when he stepped out of the shower?' Ahem.

(Earlier we'd been introduced to the Rams' marketing direc-tor—the famed former player Jack Youngblood. He spoke to us for twenty minutes, all the time chewing tobacco. Berne was again on hand with the pertinent question: 'Jack, can you get lung cancer from chewing tobacco?')

The last person to board our flight for Bermuda via New York the next day was Stanislaus Pilecki. 'Stan the Man' is a chain-smoker whose addiction to the weed is rivalled only by that of former Wallaby coach, Bob Templeton. As he walked down the aisle a stern announcement was made: 'Ladies and gentlemen! Under US government regulations, because this flight is less than six hours, there will be *no* smoking on board.' SPRUNG!

Nevertheless, Stan was determined to have one last 'drag' before boarding—even if it made him perilously late. Wearing his Akubra hat, he finally arrived at his seat only to find it occu-pied by an attractive young lady. 'Would all passengers please be seated, thank you!' commanded the aircraft intercom.

Stan reached for the overhead compartment, opened it and the entire contents came tumbling down on the unsuspecting female.

Pilecki was most apologetic as he slowly and methodically retrieved the articles from her lap. You just can't take prop forwards *anywhere* without provoking an international incident! When Stan had finally finished re-stowing the locker, he was found a seat way down the back in between two little old ladies—whom he entertained with rugby stories for the entire journey.

A three-hour stopover in New York followed. Some of the lads had enjoyed the bright lights of Los Angeles to the detriment of their 'beauty sleep', a deficit they endeavoured to make good by taking a nap in the JFK transit lounge. Two such cases were former NSW Country centre Billy 'Snake-bite' McKidd and Parramatta winger Mick Martin. A headcount by tour organiser Gary Pearse after we'd boarded for the last leg to Bermuda revealed two missing Wallabies. Billy, a farmer from Barraba in northwest NSW, was dead to the world on the floor of the departure lounge, as was his mate the Central Coast roof tiler!

A frantic Pearse called out to a cabin attendant as the aircraft door had already been closed. It was a minor masterpiece of improvised white-lying: 'I'm the manager of the Australian Rugby Union team and we're playing a Test match tomorrow in Bermuda and two of our star players are still in the terminal.' The flight superintendent was summoned and after much pleading an announcement was made over the aircraft public address system:

'Ladies and gentlemen! We ask for your co-operation. Due to unforeseen circumstances this flight is overbooked and two ticketed passengers from the Australian Rugby Team are still in the terminal. We need two passengers currently on board to give up their seats. In return, Continental will fly you to Bermuda tomorrow plus give you $500 cash and a return flight to anywhere in the United States. If you wish to accept the offer would you please notify the hostess immediately.'

In a flash our senior prop, Stuart 'The Runt' MacDougall, stood up. As I've already explained, you just can't take a prop forward *anywhere*. Sanity prevailed. We managed to convince 'The Runt' that it might be better if he stuck with the team. Meanwhile, an eager elderly couple accepted the airline's generous offer. Shortly afterwards, two embarrassed Wallabies trudged down the aisle—to the rousing cheers of their comrades.

Bermuda at last. Spotless houses painted mainly in whites, light blues and cream. The ocean a sparkling turquoise blue. Palm trees and rum. The island had a friendly, seductive feel. What better setting for a band of ageing ex-Wallabies!

The Classics tournament itself is a wonderful concept—one big party under the guise of a rugby tournament. But importantly, it brings together rugby legends from around the globe. For me it offered some incredible experiences, like eavesdropping on a conversation between Stan Pilecki and the famed Pontypool duo of Graham Price and Charlie Faulkner. And who could forget (even if they wanted to) the cabaret night when 'Topo' Rodriguez stripped down to his speedos in a seductive performance which for some obscure reason required him to walk across thirty-five crowded tables?

In the tournament, the Classic Wallabies were knocked out in the semi-final by Wales, but not before Pilecki tested Graham Price's jaw early on (in what could only be described as a symbolic gesture). J.P.R. Williams caused havoc with his sorties from fullback while J.J. Williams simply had a bit too much toe for a well-nourished Mick Martin. In the second half skipper Mark Loane called for a do-or-die effort—which promptly resulted in Stuart MacDougall being carted off on a stretcher after colliding with one of his own goalposts.

And then, in the best Hollywood tradition of *A Star is Born*, my fleeting moment of glory arrived.

Fifteen minutes from full-time I came on at scrum-half to

replace a fatigued Peter Carson. A Wallaby at last! Immediately—even before my treasured green and gold jersey could collect its first spot of mud—my opponent, Brynmor Williams, gave me a welcoming clip across the ear. I dutifully reported this indiscretion to the referee and gained our side a welcome penalty.

All too soon my stint of representative honours was over, but I'd played just enough rugby in the national colours to justify hours of tedious reminiscences to be endured by my children and grandchildren.

In the final, Wales were no match for those all-too-bloody-serious Kiwis skippered by Andy Haden. True to form, that team had been on a full-scale internal tour of New Zealand as part of their preparation for the tournament. Well guys, it's only a game, but if you want it *that* much . . .

In truth, the results weren't really important to the majority of the Classics participants. As that oft-quoted rugby motto says, 'we were there for a good time, not a long time'. The tour certainly delivered on its promises and was every burnt-out prop forward's ultimate fantasy: palm trees, cocktails and no pushing in the scrums.

• •

The celebrated Russian winger Prince Alexander Obolensky is best remembered for his glorious two-try performance in England's famous 13–0 victory over the All Blacks in 1936. Obolensky lived a short, swashbuckling and typically Russian life. The Prince studied at Oxford and still holds the world individual scoring record for a single representative match—an incredible 17 tries for the RFU against Brazil in 1936. Capped just four times, Obolensky was the first rugby international to lose his life during WWII. He died during training as a fighter pilot.

• •

The celebrated English sporting brothers Edward and Sir George Turner both played for their country during the late 1870s, were both forwards, and were both doctors. Edward, however, was also an accomplished cyclist. He held all the tricycle world records from 2 to 25 miles, and was able to better all the bicycle times over the same distances. That level of pedal power must have been useful in the scrums.

An Inauspicious Debut

Not many of us can brush aside an initial disaster to establish a new career in a single afternoon. But rugby players good enough to represent their country are hewn from special wood—and deserve some special protection.

THERE'S no mistaking the tall frame and cocker spaniel eyes of Gary Pearse, one-time Executive Director of the New South Wales Rugby Union. At six feet four inches (194 cms) he was tall timber even for a flanker. Twenty years ago his ball skills and aggression were good enough to see him in the sacred green and gold packing down with Mark Loane and Tony Shaw against legends such as Gary Knight and the immortal Andy Haden.

I suppose his exalted status in rugby administration was living proof that some forwards must have managed at least a 'pass' at the end of kindergarten before their first scrum, but GP wasn't always such a smoothie. Long before 'Treasure the ball!' became his catchcry, 'Pearsy' enjoyed fleeting fame for his role in a moment of broadcasting we'd both prefer to forget.

My association with fellow-commentator Gareth Keith Pearse

goes back to the disappointing Wallaby tour of France in 1976. In an uncharacteristic display of zeal, he managed to do too many sit-ups in training before the first game at Toulon and strained his groin. In fact, he ended up spending most of that four-week campaign on the sideline.

A (not very) civil engineer by profession, Gary had impressed me with his ability to communicate 'ad lib' the structure of a rugby contest as it unfolded before our eyes. I'd discovered this happy knack when using him as an 'unofficial' expert during practice calls we did for the lead-up matches to the first Test.

GP's only major drawback then was that he invariably succumbed to the understandable temptation of barracking for his team-mates. If the Australian winger was charging for the line it usually became (over the top of my description): '*Go Paddy, Go!*' (Winger Paddy Batch made many such thrilling runs on the tour.) Pearsy swore on a stack of French bibles that he would restrain his partisanship for the 'real' broadcasts.

Gary's baptism of fire as a commentator was to be the first Test at Bordeaux in the heart of red wine country. The ABC Radio team was ready to meet the challenge. Our broadcasting 'possie' was slap-bang in the middle of the main grandstand, surrounded by what seemed like a full battalion of well-lubricated, noisy, garlic-breathing local supporters. To make matters worse, the bored technician supplied by Radio France could not comprehend what survived of my schoolboy French—or didn't want to. We had no idea if the call was even reaching its destination in Australia.

So, in the best traditions of sports commentators the world over, there was nothing for it except to 'press on in hope'. As luck would have it the match started badly for the Wallabies. The opposition backs cut loose and the French had run in two tries within the first ten minutes. Their fullback kicked both conversions so we found ourselves trailing 12–0—a try being still worth only four points—with the Test barely underway. It looked like being a long, depressing afternoon.

But the Wallabies were far from done for. Slowly the forwards began to achieve parity and, at least in our judgment, seemed to be finishing the half with the upper hand. Then, just before the break, outside centre Ken Wright launched a scything attack.

'He's around Bertranne ... what a side-step! Only fullback Droitecourt in front ... here comes Monaghan! He takes the pass ... and that's the try that puts Australia back in business!' After a short burst of (strictly impartial) cheering from Pearsy, I jumped back in: 'Oh no! Referee Alan Hosie has ruled "forward pass" and he was at least twenty metres behind the play. I don't believe it.' Gary's comment, which reverberated around Australia on the national radio network, was a trifle more succinct:

'*BULLSHIT!*'

At the time, this particular exclamation was not generally used in the local media, and certainly not on Talbot Duckmanton's ABC. Visions of a glorious career shattered before my eyes. This was my first rugby tour—and now, perhaps, my last.

Australia went on to lose that match 18–15, and needless to say Monaghan's disallowed try would have reversed that result. To add to our misery I discovered that night that the broadcast had been received clear as a bell back home, complete with the aforementioned gratuitous contribution from Mr Pearse. When the inevitable phone call came from my then boss, the late Bert Oliver, I was prepared:

'Bert, before you say anything, I've told that supporter to keep right away from our microphones in future.'

We got away with it. Gary soon went back to being a Wallaby but later rejoined me in the commentary box and his career blossomed. Not once did he repeat that first reference to the byproduct of bovine bowel evacuation. But, whenever he had a go at me about my referring to Concord Oval instead of the pompous 'Waratah Rugby Park', I reminded Pearsy that it's unlikely he'll *ever* be able to repay me for my initiative and loyalty back in 1976.

A freak incident on the field during the 1996 NSW v Queensland game rekindled memories of the way in which inventive players have always been able to bend the laws of rugby for fun and profit.

Generations ago, the famous star Dally Messenger out-thought the rule-makers with his intentional throw forward. At the time, Messenger's trick of lobbing the ball over a defender and then catching it again was considered legal. His trademark 'Dally Lob' yielded many tries before the law was eventually changed.

In their incredible last-gasp 1996 win Queensland's David Wilson may have invented the 'Header from Heaven'.

Two minutes into injury time, Wilson accidentally headed the ball forward before regathering and going on to deliver the winning pass to Jason Little. A knock-on can only occur when some part of the arm makes contact with the ball, so Wilson's action was therefore quite legitimate.

Various intriguing possibilties spring to mind. For example, how about 'Slippery' John Eales balancing the ball on his head for a touch-line run, then flicking it over the opposing backs before regathering like a trained seal?

Nah. All sounds like too much of a headache.

Cup Eve

On the eve of the 1991 World Cup opener between England and New Zealand I did a television interview for the ABC with the ground superintendent at Twicken- ham, a Mr Ken Cox. Regrettably, it was never broadcast, due to time constraints on the big day. An hour later that disappointment was extinguished when my passion for fossicking among the trivia of obscure rugby facts bore profitable fruit.

MR COX explained how he'd followed the same ritual at Twickenham for twenty-five years. Every Thursday evening before an International he draped the England jumpers across three pegs in the dressing room, upside down and numbers facing out. Except for the last two jumpers—numbers 'one' and 'two'. 'Why was that?' I enquired.

'Well, before the players arrive on match day, committee members like to bring guests down to see the orderly rooms to soak up the atmosphere. And I always leave the last shirt front out because the ladies find the red rose most inviting. If only they saw the rooms after the game.'

To think that England front rowers have been closet sex symbols all these years! Mr Cox also revealed how the seven baths in each dressing room were run with boiling water two hours before kick-off to a level of nine to twelve inches (22–30 cms) so that the temperature would be just right when the players returned after the game.

Suddenly he became a little emotional. 'My greatest joy is when the England members are sharing a victory. Two, sometimes three players lolling in each bath smoking cigars and drinking French champagne.' He then swallowed before continuing. 'I sincerely hope it's England's turn. But I have the feeling the celebrations will be in the visitors' rooms tomorrow.'

I could have killed my producers when they told me the interview had been dropped. But consolation was close at hand.

The Italians had certainly been one of the big improvers in the previous World Cup. Back in 1987 they'd conceded fifty-three points in the second half alone against New Zealand, including one extravagant effort by John Kirwan which took him on a ninety-metre journey through their entire team. No such embarrassments in 1991. The Italians actually outscored New Zealand in the second half 18–15 before going down 31–21.

But the point of this story isn't Italy's strong resurgence but a touch of *déjà vu* regarding that World Cup debut in 1987. Their clash with New Zealand had been the first Cup game. Four years later, on the eve of England's opener against the All Blacks, my research uncovered a significant but little-known fact. Michael Jones had actually scored the first *individual* try of that first World Cup. (The actual first score was a penalty try to the Kiwis awarded by Australian referee Bob Fordham.) Here was an omen indeed!

As a man who's always enjoyed a flutter I headed down to William Hill's bookmaking shop. There was Jones's name quoted at 20–1 to score the first try again. I promptly handed over ten pounds and then thought, 'No, make it twenty'—remembering a shyster mate who'd once told me: 'The longer the price, the more you put on 'em!'.

It's now part of rugby folklore that Michael Jones secured the first try of the 1991 World Cup just after half-time. Nick Farr-Jones has always accused me of getting carried away whenever David Campese received the ball. He felt the other Aussie backs were suffering something of a raw deal from this commentator. I'm quite sure he has a point. However, according to the only other person who knew about the bet on Jones—my wife Cathy watching the telecast back in Sydney—my description of his try reached new heights of fervour and enthusiasm.

And I'm happy to confess that this was one occasion on which I was delighted to see the All Blacks draw first blood on a rugby field.

• •

During their build-up for the 1987 World Cup, the All Blacks enlisted the military for specialist support.

The problem was that their scrum machine kept moving backwards during a training session at Burnham Camp. A sturdy army truck was summoned to park in front of the machine and resist the New Zealand pack.

The solution had the desired effect. After the Scots went down 30–3 their famous fifty-two-cap hooker Colin Deans described the All Black scrum as the best he'd ever played against.

• •

The historical sporting curiosity of Australia's Olympic gold medal for rugby at the London Games in 1908 is well documented.

The Wallabies beat English County champions Cornwall, representing the UK, 32–3, but only after surviving a half-time protest from a Pommy official who reckoned our lads were wearing running spikes.

But what is not commonly known about that contest is that we could never have done worse than the silver medal.

Australia and Cornwall were the only two teams to take part.

The Commentating Caper

It's a highly sought-after occupation, which is hardly surprising because you get paid for doing something you truly love. After nearly thirty years spent behind microphones all over Australia and the world (and at nearly every type of sporting event imaginable), perhaps it's time to share a few home truths about this curious trade of mine, the commentating caper.

TO BEGIN at the beginning. I was not long out of school and had somehow survived to be included in the final shortlist of three contenders for the position of 'Specialist Trainee, ABC Sport'. The last interview in the selection process comprised a studio test for reading ability, ad-libbing and sports general knowledge. This trial was to be conducted by a young Drew Morphett, who'd only just graduated from the sports trainee ranks himself.

Drew fired twenty questions at me on tape after which he declared, 'Look, Gordon, you've done pretty well but the opposition is bloody hot. A puck is not used in curling—it's the bloody pill in ice hockey!' He then corrected me on two other misses before explaining he was going to re-spool the tape and start again. Who was I to argue? (And naturally I didn't ask any questions). At the completion of the exercise Drew promised, 'Mum's the word, mate.'

But why did he do that for me? I couldn't resist asking.

'Because I reckon you're the best man for the job. On your way, mate, and I hope it all works out.' Thanks, Drew. We all need a helping hand at some stage and I believe Drew's leg-up must have given me the decisive edge. After all, 100 per cent on a sporting general knowledge test is hard to beat ...

For the record, Andrew Morphett combines part-time commentating with cattle-breeding these days. He's best known for his colourful AFL and Olympic broadcasts for the Seven Network. But in his ABC days (and notwithstanding his generosity at the beginning of my career), we caught him out beautifully one afternoon at the MCG during a cricket Test between Australia and Pakistan.

For reasons not unconnected with his active social life, Drew had managed little sleep the night before and duly dozed off in the commentary box during an 'off-duty' period in the morning session. Our alert television director quietly moved a camera from outside to record Morphett in slumber mode.

Later that afternoon, in a brief break in play, the tape was replayed 'on air' in the middle of Drew's commentary stint. Alan Hurst, Jack Potter and myself were all hanging over his shoulder at the magic moment. There, for every Australian cricket lover to see, was Drew waking up from his morning doze—in ultra-slow motion, and before his very eyes. Was this a nightmare? The look of sheer mortification when he turned towards us was memorable. A flurry of choice expletives followed—beautifully enunciated, but not *uttered*.

So, *Lesson One* in the broadcasters' manual: Always keep your guard up.

In those formative years one of my senior colleagues was the then 'Voice of Soccer', Martin Royal. A delightful chap with a beautifully modulated voice, Marty's enthusiasm for his beloved round-ball code made a big impression on me. I vividly recall sitting alongside him for a World Cup qualifier against Korea at the old Sydney Sports Ground. (Observing senior broadcasters at work was an integral part of a trainee's education.)

At half-time Martin's instruction was to repeat the score and cross back to the studio. His closing words went something like this: 'So there we have it. An enthralling first half with Australia and Korea nil-all ...' He then paused for the regulation five or six seconds of safety silence before proceeding with the following banter to the TV director in the OB truck: ... 'Oh, David dear boy. Have I got time to go for a leak?' Apparently, Norman May, who was anchoring the telecast back at the Gore Hill studios was answering a similar call of nature at precisely the same moment and wasn't there to take his cue. So Martin's plaintive request was heard by every soccer fan in Australia and, as we were later informed, in South Korea as well!

Lesson Two: Always assume the microphone is 'live', and,

Lesson Three: Always have a comfort stop before a telecast.

One of the delights of the old ABC was that most production staff could expect some enjoyable periods of 'secondment' service in other States. This tradition was both practical and long-sighted in terms of career development. It not only plugged gaps caused by illness, resignations or holidays, but also allowed broadcasters the opportunity for promotion and to work in new environments, broaden their range of professional contacts and learn new sports.

My first major interstate transfer was to Tasmania, and was never short on variety. One of my initial assignments was to cover a lawn bowls tournament in Launceston with the 'North' playing the 'South'. In Tasmania such contests are taken very seriously indeed. It was the dawn of the new colour television era, so we devised a system of coloured discs which were stuck on the sides of the bowls to help the viewers follow the competition. Carefully rehearsed introductory lines were firmly implanted in my memory for the live cross from Hobart. The big moment finally arrived and my adrenalin was pumping.

'Welcome to Launceston. It's intra-state rivalry as the North takes on the South. May I now introduce the two skips, Dave Vincent from Launceston and Michael Lester from Hobart. And incidentally, you can distinguish between the two bowlers because Dave has yellow spots on his balls!' I realised something had possibly gone amiss when the cameraman fell backwards from his viewfinder and rolled about on the green in hysterics. But my training and instincts told me to just keep going.

Lesson Four: Never highlight a mistake.

Still in Tasmania, this nascent sports broadcaster was then faced with the prospect of providing 'live' commentary for a contest which fell well outside the normal repertoire of televised sports. The sum total of my experience in woodchopping was confined to glimpses of the burly axemen through wisps of fairy floss as a child on the annual family visit to the Royal Easter Show. But to a cocky young ABC lad, calling those same world champions hacking up logs at the Devonport Show seemed like a piece of cake. Just one small problem. Our commentary position was in the centre of the ground, but the axemen in the first heat were facing the grandstand with their backs to us. I was handed the draw, which numbered the contestants one-to-seven, from the left.

Off they went, chips flying everywhere and the crowd roaring encouragement. After the first blow I realised my commentary had also been switched to the public address system, producing a one-and-a-half second delay in my ears. Rattled but still focused I pressed on, confidently building excitement and expectation with my descriptive flow. That confidence, however, was badly shaken when an agitated show official came sprinting across to our broadcast point waving his hands and shaking his head. Clearly something was wrong, but I kept going until Doug Youd struck the winning blow. As the applause faded I was handed a scribbled note which told me what you've already guessed—I had the contestants' places back-to-front. They were numbered one-to-seven—but facing the grandstand!

By chance, however, I emerged from the fiasco with some of my dignity intact. Because Youd was chopping on stand four—and in a field of seven stand four was in the middle—I'd at least managed to get the winner right! Caught up in the excitement of the event, I'm sure the majority of spectators were oblivious to my error.

Lesson Five: Keep the faith and say everything with conviction.

Life in Hobart for a young commentator was never dull, particularly if you were trying to keep up an active sporting life yourself. The only trouble was that during the weekend the ABC needed all hands on deck for the job of covering sport, but weekends were also the time when young blokes like me wanted to be out on the field playing sport themselves. During the summer months I devised a devious scheme whereby I could discharge my professional duties but also indulge my other sporting passion—cricket.

Saturday mornings were supposed to be spent in the ABC office cutting out the local and interstate race fields from the newspaper for the afternoon omnibus-style sports show (which has since evolved into *Grandstand*). After that tedious chore was complete it was usually time to depart to cover your allocated sporting event for the afternoon. We described everything from ten-pin bowling to horse trials.

Ever resourceful, I used to work back on Friday nights cutting and pasting, which left me free to play cricket for the Associates Rugby Club on Saturday mornings. My boss wasn't aware of these regular escapades and certainly wouldn't have approved because the race fields in the Friday papers were missing over half the jockeys. Fortunately, the sympathetic sports show announcers filled in my blanks from the Saturday editions.

For almost two seasons this stratagem worked like a dream. In the second year Associates played well but we still had to win our last match against the top side to make the semi-finals. Normally I'd manage to get away at midday—an hour before stumps. However, on that particular day it simply wasn't possible. We needed ninety-one runs for victory in forty minutes.

For young Mr Bray there was another small problem—I was due on air at the Huon River—a good hour's drive away—no later than 1.30 p.m. to call the feature event of the State Power Boating Championships. The situation was desperate. I opened the innings and runs flowed. After much good fortune I managed to survive until 12.55 by which stage just ten more runs were needed in what was a life-or-death struggle for Associates cricket club as well. Press on! The semi-final spot was within reach! Unfortunately I was bowled first ball of what turned out to be the last over—we failed by just five runs. But now the *real* mercy dash was on.

Driving like a madman, I arrived at the Huon at around 1.55 p.m. only to discover that the main race was already in progress. After frantically searching for the radio position, I got to the microphone just as the winning boat crossed the line. So much for our live broadcast of the blue riband event of the championships.

My career was rapidly unravelling before my eyes like the plot of a B-grade movie and I had to do something desperate to retrieve it. After a hurried conference with a spectator who kindly let me have his program, I called the next race live to air—but *as if* it was the main event. Could I get away with this outrageous deception? We had the right sound effects and the same course—

just different boats and drivers. Surely only the most discerning 'petrol head' would detect the much lower horsepower engine notes. *Mea maxima culpa*, but to this day no-one in ABC Sport has been any the wiser.

Lesson Six: Follow the heart against duty at your own peril.

The Brisbane Commonwealth Games in 1982 was one of the most inspiring projects I've worked on. They produced record ratings for the ABC and the style of the television coverage, devised by executive producers Dick Mason and Robbie Weekes, proved a real winner. Commentators crossed to each other between venues to maximise the spontaneity of this exciting 'live' coverage. Daytime studio host Peter Meares was used sparingly yet effectively, mainly updating results, introducing features and conducting studio interviews.

At the time it was a revolutionary approach. Commercial television quickly adopted this style for big international events, but the format doesn't always work so well for them because of time zone considerations and interruptions for advertising breaks.

I was lucky enough to be the prime-time evening studio host for the Games coverage, but it still didn't save me from one of my most embarrassing moments. Late each day of the Games 'Mearesy' and I had to manage a hasty changeover in the studio. We had just sixty seconds to swap positions before I did a short promotional break leading into the seven o'clock news.

Everything was proceeding as usual one evening during the second week. Operation Swapover had been successfully carried out and all was in readiness.

'Cue Gordon!' I responded to the floor-manager's signal and began telling millions of Australians what delights awaited them. For a full forty-five seconds I delivered this spiel on national television until I caught sight of a technician holding up a lapel microphone. Mearesy had left the studio still wearing the bloody thing! I'd inserted my earpiece but forgotten the most important piece of equipment of all. In the industry the result is known as the 'goldfish' effect: the viewers are treated to energetic lip movement, but without sound. Let me assure you that the effect on the goldfish is devastating.

Lesson Seven: Always ensure the horse is before the cart.

Olympic and Commonwealth Games have produced some memorable one-liners from the commentators. A brief selection:

Herb Elliot, after Raylene Boyle won the 400 metres and then did a swansong lap of honour. 'I don't know what she's feeling down there but I'm certainly feeling it up here.' (What was that again, Herb?)

Dick Mason, covering Olympic basketball after a decision went against the Australian men's team. 'This referee is either incompetent or a cheat and I suspect it's the latter.' (Amazingly, no defamation suit ensued.)

Tim Lane, calling the Games marathon in Brisbane. 'The two Tanzanians are taking it in turns to break wind out in front.' (Later in the race they literally passed water—the Brisbane River.)

Norman May, on Michael Gross before an Olympic final. 'This man swims like a greyhound!' (... and runs like a shark?)

Norman May, again on the art of gaining a winning edge. 'The thing about backstroke is not to actually go before the gun but to anticipate the gun and try and go just before it.' (Glad we've cleared that up, Nugget.)

Phil May, before a critical attempt in the women's long jump at the Brisbane Games: 'If she hits the board and *bangs* a big one, she'll be in the bronze medal position.' (Phil didn't go on to *describe* the position.)

Gordon Bray, covering track and field at the Edmonton Games: 'Fortunately we're shitting in the sade. I beg your pardon, shitting in the shade!' (*Much* better.)

Lesson Eight: Whenever possible (and there are many times when it's not), *think* before you speak.

The 42 kilometres of a marathon race are perhaps the greatest test of an athletics commentator. The event usually involves scores of runners, traverses awkward terrain for broadcasting, and takes around two-and-a-half hours to complete. I covered my first Australian Marathon in Hobart in the early seventies. It was to be an engrossing head-to-head clash between the then world record-holder Derek Clayton from Victoria and the impressive New South Welshman, John Farrington.

This was a major assignment because my brief was to provide a 'simulcast commentary'—the one description to be used for radio and television simultaneously. (All my colleagues were doing Aussie Rules throughout the weekend, leaving the whole job to me.) The sophisticated coverage plan was for me to call the start and then hop in my car and drive to designated vantage points along the route to pick up the commentary again. Despite these daunting logistics the boss insisted I still complete the afore-mentioned horse race cut-and-paste job in the office before rushing off to the start. I made it with just a few minutes to spare before the gun. I'd researched and prepared for the event over the previous three days, but there was no time now to familiarise myself with the runners.

What followed can only be described as a broadcaster's worst nightmare. I'm sure it must have happened to every commentator at some stage in their careers, but why *me*? For some inexplicable reason I confused the two star competitors. My brain was somehow locked into an image of Derek Clayton's face belonging to John Farrington, and vice versa. In hindsight the lapse is still unbelievable. I was reasonably familiar with both men, having seen them run individually at other events. But when the big moment arrived, that dreadful mental block took over.

So, for almost the entire 42.195 kilometres I had the two

champions the wrong way around. Fortunately the pair spent more than two hours running shoulder-to-shoulder until Clayton made his winning break a couple of kilometres from the finish. Even the logistics of the simulcast had gone smoothly. Incredibly, my old Austin Freeway had started first-go every time as I scrambled between each commentary point. Finally I was ensconced above the finish line in the main grandstand of the Glenorchy Showgrounds, waiting for the leader to appear on the trotting track. When he did I really 'put the foot down', knowing my radio call was going to the mainland and on the national network.

'We're set for a monumental upset here in the Australian Marathon Championship. John Farrington, in a decisive move, gave world number one Derek Clayton the slip just one mile from home. What a performance and what a breakthrough for the New South Welshman . . .' At that moment, an elderly gentleman sitting alongside me abruptly jabbed his elbow into my ribcage. Within earshot of my microphone and probably the national audience he barked: 'You bloody idiot. That's Clayton, not Farrington!'

It remains the most galling moment of my entire broadcasting career. In a twinkling the penny finally dropped and a shattered young ABC commentator continued. 'Yes, and what a sensational performance by the world champion Derek Clayton. As I was saying, he made that decisive move . . .'

Lesson Nine: Attend the training sessions. Always meet and talk to the athletes before their event.

Six long passages south on the Radio Relay Vessel covering the Sydney–Hobart yacht race have yielded many fond memories. That is, until my last voyage, in 1984. The record fleet that year was pounded by fierce conditions which caused an astonishing 103 retirements. On the second night at sea aboard the *Wyuna* we received the dreaded 'Mayday' call from a stricken yacht, *Yahoo II*. The veteran Lake Macquarie yachtsman Wal

Russell was missing overboard. The Hobart race organisers were justifiably proud of their safety record. No competitor had ever been lost at sea. Russell's disappearance caused a sensation. My nightly sports report suddenly became a major news story. We were in the search area but in frightening seas. Yachts were being dismasted and knocked over like nine-pins.

Writing a ten-minute script in a decidedly unfriendly seaway, trying to remain both informative and creative, and then broadcasting the result from a vessel tossing about in the Tasman comes close to being the ultimate challenge for a commentator. Bracing myself between rolls, I adopted a technique of rushing to complete just one line of script before the crest of the next wave crashed over us.

Normally the finished report was transmitted to the ABC about twenty minutes before scheduled air-time. This covered any contingencies such as reception problems or unplanned interruptions for the sudden onset of seasickness ('Sorry, listeners, we had a brief technical problem'). Under the dramatic circumstances of the 1984 race, radio operator Bert Oliver—himself a senior broadcaster with the ABC—sent a message through to me from the radio room that we would now be going out live. At 9.40 p.m., ten minutes before the scheduled transmission, I decided it was time to head down from the bridge to the broadcast point at the stern of *Wyuna*.

It turned out to be a hazardous exercise, and almost a fatal one. As I made a dash across the slippery deck, we were hit broadside by a gigantic wave. The ship did a 38-degree roll, which is about as close as you come to capsizing a motor yacht. I was swept from my feet in a furious surge of seawater before crashing into a lifeboat. I'll never forget my sense of helplessness against the power of the ocean during those fleeting moments. I also remember thinking, 'This is it, pal!'

But as the ship righted I somehow managed to scramble to my

feet and lunged at the door handle of the radio room. As I staggered inside, soaked to the skin and apparently as white as a ghost, Bert snapped at me, 'Christ! Where have you been?' He noticed that I'd arrived without a script—the pages had been torn from my hand and washed overboard by the wave.

'I'll ad-lib it, Bert,' came my reply.

'No you bloody won't. Get back to the bridge and get into some dry clothes. I'll see you in the morning.'

Bert Oliver was a mentor and father figure to me. He told me next day I'd suffered shock and was in no state to broadcast. He was right, but I still felt as though I'd let a lot of people down. Throughout that night, Bert co-ordinated the *Wyuna*'s search effort for Wal Russel, but it proved a forlorn exercise.

I soon regained my composure and worked a large searchlight from the bridge, hoping for that million-to-one chance of catching sight of the faint glow of reflective wet weather gear in the dark, boiling seas. Occasionally our eyes would play tricks but sadly the terrible emptiness remained.

Later, when there was time to reflect on my narrow escape, I decided in the early morning hours that 1984 would be my last Sydney–Hobart.

Lesson Ten: After all the travel and adventure is said and done, self-preservation is the ultimate rule in the broadcasters' manual.

The author wishes to thank those who contributed to the following publications which have been reference points for statistics and anecdotes:

Australian Rugby—The Game and the Players, Jack Pollard, Pan MacMillan, 1994

Encyclopaedia of World Rugby, Keith Quinn, ABC Books, 1991

The Legends of Springbok Rugby, D.H. Craven and Keith Clayton, KC Publications, 1989

Men in Black, R.H. Chester and N.A.C. McMillan, Moa Publications, 1978

Spirit of Rugby, G.T. Bray (ed), HarperSports, 1995

The Visitors, R.H. Chester and N.A.C. McMillan, Moa Publications, 1978

Who's Who of International Rugby, Terry Godwin, Blandford Press, 1987

Nick Farr-Jones
Peter FitzSimons

2 November 1991—the Wallabies stand at the pinnacle of world rugby union. Nick-Farr-Jones holds aloft the World Cup—the symbol of rugby supremacy.

Journalist and former Wallaby Peter FitzSimons answers the questions which lie behind the making of a master sportsman. He takes us from Farr-Jones' early days as the least athletically gifted of three brothers, through his days at Newington College (where he could only make the Second XV), Sydney University, and the breakthrough into international rugby. *Nick Farr-Jones* shows how the fiercely competitive individual became the competitive team member, and an inspiring captain.

This is the fascinating background to the heady days of the Grand Slam, failure in the inaugural World Cup, triumph in the 1991 World Cup—and the satisfying victory over South Africa in 1992. FitzSimons also tells of the importance of Nick's family—especially his maternal grandfather and parents, his marriage to Angie, and his conversion to Christianity.

Nick Farr-Jones is the gripping and energetic story of both a great sportsman and the most successful period in Australian rugby.

Ian Roberts—Finding Out
Paul Freeman

With the odds stacked against him making a career out of foot-ball, and despite an injury-hampered rise in first-grade rugby league, Ian Roberts was widely acclaimed as the best front-rower in the world in the late eighties. There was acrimony and even bomb threats when he left his humble working-class South Sydney surrounds to play with the 'silvertail' club Manly in 1989, a move that made him league's highest-paid player ever at the time.

Three years later he was broke and broken.

By 1995, having once again overcome insurmountable odds, and amidst further controversy, he signed with Rupert Mur-doch's Super League, while seeing out his commitment to the ARL flagship club Manly. That year he was almost crippled with a knee injury, but played through to the grand final.

At the same time he became arguably the world's first high profile sportsman to voluntarily confirm his much-rumoured homosexuality, subjecting himself once again to the litany of abuse that has seemed to follow his every move. This time, however, there was the acclaim and certainty that he had done great good and that right was on his side. And with that knowl-edge and the support of scores of admirers and mentors came the peace and happiness that had eluded Ian for so long.

This is his story, told in his own words, but also told by friends, family and team-mates, the story of an ordinary man with an extraordinary talent and the courage to live his life the way he wants to.

Ten Years in Black and White
Crackers Keenan

'Don't go to Collingwood, Crackers, they're bastards down there,' were Jack Dyer's first words when he heard about Crackers' decision to join Collingwood.

Lucky for us, Crackers didn't listen to Jack or his wife, Judy. In his inimitable manner, and for the first time ever, Crackers spills the beans and pulls the skeletons out of the Collingwood closet.

Find out how Collingwood overcame the Colliwobbles to win the 1990 Grand Final. Get the lowdown on Peter Daicos and Tony Shaw. What does Crackers really think about Dermie's body? How does the Collingwood rumour mill work?

Grab a hot pie and tinnie, sit back, and enjoy all these and more in *Ten Years in Black and White*.

Crackers Keenan is a legend. An AFL player and coach, TV and radio commentator, horse-racing nut and author of *Dead Certs and Dog Food*, he is about to rock the AFL to its roots with the warts-and-all story of Collingwood.

Dead Certs and Dog Food
Crackers Keenan

For a jockey, Crackers Keenan was a pretty good footballer.

But as a punter and racehorse owner, he's been kicking goals all his life.

Peter 'Crackers' Keenan, former Aussie Rules footballer and now commentator and media larrikin, has always loved the punt. From the time he was knee-high to Roy Higgins, horse have been his passion. Breeding, training, racing, betting . . . you name it, Crackers has been in the thick of it.

And after a lifetime in the racing scene, he has a swag of stories as thick as a bookie's bag.

From the great trainers like Bart Cummings and Tommy Smith to the wonderful and weird world of the jockey; from champion horses to the donkeys who couldn't win a one-horse race if they tried, Crackers has worked—and laughed—with them all.

Now, with *Dead Certs and Dog Food*, Crackers, in his inimitable style gives you the mail on Australia's funniest racing yarns.

Ringside
Edited by Peter Corris and Barry Parish

This collection of boxing includes fiction and non-fiction from the past to the present day. A must for every fight fan! Great writers like Ernest Hemingway, Jack London, Damon Runyon, Martin Cruz Smith, P.G. Wodehouse, Australia's Murray Bail and Jeff Wells, plus the words of the great boxers themselves, such as Jack Johnson and Johnny Famechon telling their stories.

Here are legendary fights down the ages, from one-on-one contests in the time of Homer, to the heyday of bare-knuckle prize-fighting in the nineteenth century, to the superstars of boxing today. All the big names are here: Les Darcy, Joe Louis, Sugar Ray Robinson, Jeff Fenech, Mike Tyson, Muhammad Ali and more.

A knockout collection of fights and fighters: the winners, the losers, the legends.